BILLY
GRAHAM
Evangelistic Assoc
Always Good Ne

Dear Friend,

I am pleased to send you this copy of C.H. Spurgeon's book *Grace: God's Unmerited Favor.*

A powerful writer, Spurgeon helps us better understand the riches of our salvation. *"Because of his grace given you in Christ Jesus ... you have been enriched in every way"* (1 Corinthians 1:4–5, NIV). Through God's unmerited favor, He has given His children unconditional love, pardon for sin, everlasting life, and so much more. Best of all, we don't have to earn them—they're part of our inheritance in Christ. I pray you'll find new peace and purpose for living as you discover the many promises of God's grace found in His Word.

For nearly 60 years the Billy Graham Evangelistic Association has worked to take the Good News of Jesus Christ throughout the world by every effective means available, and I'm excited about what God will do in the years ahead.

We would appreciate knowing how our ministry has touched your life. May God bless you.

Sincerely,

Franklin Graham
President

If you would like to know more about our ministry, please contact us:

In the U.S.:

Billy Graham Evangelistic Association
1 Billy Graham Parkway
Charlotte, NC 28201-0001
billygraham.org
info@bgea.org
Toll-free: 1-877-2GRAHAM (1-877-247-2426)

In Canada:

Billy Graham Evangelistic Association of Canada
20 Hopewell Way NE
Calgary, AB T3J 5H5
billygraham.ca
Toll-free: 1-888-393-0003

GRACE
GOD'S UNMERITED
FAVOR

C. H. Spurgeon

This *Billy Graham Library Selection* is published for
the Billy Graham Evangelistic Association
by Whitaker House.

WHITAKER
HOUSE

A *Billy Graham Library Selection* designates materials that are appropriate for a well-rounded collection of quality Christian literature, including both classic and contemporary reading and reference materials.

This *Billy Graham Library Selection* is published for the Billy Graham Evangelistic Association by Whitaker House.

Publisher's note: This new edition from Whitaker House is a revision of the complete original text. The resulting version has been edited for content and also updated for the modern reader. Words, expressions, and sentence structure have been revised for clarity and readability.

All Scripture quotations are taken from the King James Version of the Holy Bible.

GRACE: GOD'S UNMERITED FAVOR

ISBN: 978-1-60374-237-5
Previous ISBN: 978-0-88368-956-1
Printed in the United States of America
©1996 by Whitaker House

Whitaker House
1030 Hunt Valley Circle
New Kensington, PA 15068
whitakerhouse.com

Contents

1. The Covenant of Grace 7

2. Salvation Altogether by Grace 31

3. Grace, the One Way of Salvation 63

4. All of Grace 91

5. Grace for the Covenanter 109

6. Twelve Covenant Mercies 141

About the Author 169

Chapter One
The Covenant of Grace

One

The Covenant
of Grace

He will ever be mindful of his covenant.
—Psalm 111:5

That God would enter into gracious covenant with men is an amazing thing. That He would create man and be gracious to man is barely conceivable. However, that God would shake hands with His creature and would subject His august majesty to an unbreakable bond with man by His own pledge is astonishing.

Once I know that God has made a covenant with man, then I am not surprised that He is mindful of it, for He is *"God, that cannot lie"* (Titus 1:2). *"Hath he said, and shall he not do it?"* (Numbers 23:19). Has He not given His promise? Thus, it is inconceivable that He would ever depart from it.

The Covenant of Grace

Our text verse commends itself to every reasonable, thoughtful man: If God has made a covenant, *"He will ever be mindful of* [that] *covenant."* For God to make a gracious covenant with us is so great a blessing that I hope everyone is saying in his heart, "Oh, may the Lord enter into covenant with me!"

I now call your attention to that point with the desire to explore it effectively. We will look into this matter by first answering the question, What is this covenant? Then, we will consider the inquiry, Am I personally included in the covenant? Finally, we will reflect on what a person's normal response to God's pledge should be: "If indeed I am in covenant with God, then every part of that covenant will be carried out, for God is ever mindful of it."

That God would create man and be gracious to man is barely conceivable.

What Is This Covenant?

If you go to a lawyer and inquire about a deed, he may reply, "I can give you a summary, but it is better if you read it thoroughly." He can tell you the essence of it; but if you want to be very accurate, and if it is a very important business, you will want to read it for yourself.

We will now read certain passages of Scripture that contain the covenant of grace, or a summary of it. First, turn to Jeremiah:

Behold, the days come, saith the LORD, *that I will make a new covenant with the house of Israel, and with the house of Judah: not according to the covenant that I made with their fathers in the day that I took them by the hand to bring them out of the land of Egypt; which my covenant they brake, although I was an husband unto them, saith the* LORD: *But this shall be the covenant that I will make with the house of Israel; after those days, saith the* LORD, *I will put my law in their inward parts, and write it in their hearts; and will be their God, and they shall be my people. And they shall teach no more every man his neighbour, and every man his brother, saying, Know the* LORD: *for they shall all know me, from the least of them unto the greatest of them, saith the* LORD: *For I will forgive their iniquity, and I will remember their sin no more.*   (Jeremiah 31:31–34)

Set every word of that in diamonds, for the significance is precious beyond measure.

Written on Hearts

God makes a covenant promise to His people that, instead of writing His law upon tablets of stone, He will write it on the tablets of their hearts. Instead of the law coming as a hard, crushing command, it will be placed within them as the object of love and delight, written on the transformed natures of His chosen, beloved people: *"I will put my law in their inward parts, and write it in their hearts."* What a covenant privilege this is!

The Covenant of Grace

A Sense of Belonging

"And [I] *will be their God."* Therefore, all that there is in God will belong to those who are in covenant with Him. *"And they shall be my people."* He is saying, "They will belong to Me; I will love them as Mine; I will keep them, bless them, honor them, and provide for them as My people. I will be their portion, and they will be My portion." What security this provides!

Heavenly Instruction

Note the next privilege. God's people will all receive heavenly instruction about a most vital point: *"They shall all know me."* Once again, God is saying, "There may be some things they do not know, but *'they shall all know me.'* They will know Me as their Father; they will know Jesus Christ as their Brother; they will know the Holy Spirit as their Comforter. They will have communion and fellowship with Me." What a privilege this is!

Forgiven and Forgotten

Then comes pardon: *"For I will forgive their iniquity, and I will remember their sin no more."* What a clean sweep of sin! God will forgive and forget; the two go together. *"I will forgive their iniquity, and I will remember their sin no more."* All their transgressions and iniquities will be blotted out, never to be mentioned against them again. What an indescribable favor!

Grace

An Unconditional Grant

This is the covenant of grace. I call your attention to the fact that there is no *if* in it; there is no *but* in it; there is no requirement of man made by it. It is all *"I will"* and *"they shall."* *"[I] will be their God, and they shall be my people."* This gracious charter is written in a royal tone, and the majestic strain is not marred by a *perhaps* or a *maybe,* but dwells always on *shall* and *will.* These are two prerogative words of the Divine Majesty. In this wondrous deed to the gift, not only does the Lord bestow a heaven of grace upon guilty sinners, but He also presents it according to the sovereignty of His own will, without anything to put the gift in jeopardy or to make the promise unsure.

> **The law will be placed within our hearts as an object of love and delight.**

More of the Covenant

Thus, we have read the covenant in one form, but if you turn a few pages in your Bible, you will come to a passage in Ezekiel. As we read, we find the bright-eyed prophet—he who lived among the wheels and the seraphim—telling us what the covenant of grace is:

> *And I will give them one heart, and I will put a new spirit within you; and I will take the stony heart out of their flesh, and will give them an heart of flesh: that*

they may walk in my statutes, and keep mine ordinances, and do them: and they shall be my people, and I will be their God. (Ezekiel 11:19–20)

You will find another form of it further on in the thirty-sixth chapter of Ezekiel. How intently you should pay attention to this! Listening to the very words of God's own covenant, a covenant that saves all those who are touched by it, is so much better than hearing any preaching of mortal man. Let us read it:

Then will I sprinkle clean water upon you, and ye shall be clean: from all your filthiness, and from all your idols, will I cleanse you. A new heart also will I give you, and a new spirit will I put within you: and I will take away the stony heart out of your flesh, and I will give you an heart of flesh. And I will put my spirit within you, and cause you to walk in my statutes, and ye shall keep my judgments, and do them. And ye shall dwell in the land that I gave to your fathers; and ye shall be my people, and I will be your God. (Ezekiel 36:25–28)

This promise always comes in at the close: *"I will be your God."* In this form of the covenant, I urge you again to witness that God demands nothing, asks no price, and exacts no payment. But, to the people with whom He enters into covenant, He makes promise after promise—all free, all unconditional, all made according to the bounty of His royal heart.

Grace

Transformed by Grace

Let us explore this in more detail. God has made a covenant with certain people that He will do all this for them, and in each case it is pure grace. He will take away their stony hearts: It is clear from the promise that, when He began with them, they had stony hearts. He will forgive their iniquities: When He began with them, they had many iniquities. He will give them hearts of flesh: When He began with them, they did not have hearts of flesh. He will teach them to keep His statutes: When He began with them, they did not keep His statutes. They were a sinful, willful, wicked, degenerate people.

God had called to them many times to come to Him and repent, but they would not. In this passage He speaks like a king, no longer pleading but instead decreeing. He declares, "I will do this and that for you, and you shall be this and that in return." Oh, blessed covenant! Oh, mighty, sovereign grace!

A Comparison of Covenants

How did all this come about? We can find out as we learn the doctrine of the two covenants.

The first covenant—made with our first father, Adam—was the covenant of works. This was not first in purpose, but it was the first to be revealed. It went like this: God Almighty declared, "Adam, you and your posterity will live and be happy *if* you will keep My law. To test your obedience to Me, there is a certain tree: *If* you leave it alone, you will live; but *if* you eat of it, you will die, as well as those whom you represent."

Our first covenant head greedily snatched at the forbidden fruit and fell. And what a fall it was, my beloved! There you and I and all of us fell, while it was proven once and for all that *"by the deeds of the law there shall no flesh be justified in his sight"* (Romans 3:20). If perfect Adam broke the law so readily, you can depend on it that you and I would break any law that God has ever made. There was no hope of happiness for any of us by a covenant that contained an *if* in it. The old covenant has been put away, for it has utterly failed. It brought nothing to us but a curse, and we are glad that it has abated and—as far as believers are concerned—has vanished away.

Then came the Second Adam. You know His name; He is the ever-blessed Son of the Highest. This Second Adam entered into covenant with God in this way: God the Father said to the Son, "I give You a people; they will be Yours. You must die to redeem them. When You have done this—when for their sakes You have kept My law and made it honorable, when for their sakes You have borne My wrath against their transgressions—then I will bless them. Then they shall be My people; I will forgive their iniquities; I will change their natures; I will sanctify them and make them perfect."

There was an apparent *if* in this covenant at first. That *if* hinged upon the question of whether Jesus would obey the law and pay the ransom, a question that His faithfulness placed beyond doubt. There is no *if* in it now. When Jesus bowed His head and said, *"It is finished"* (John 19:30), there remained no *if* in the covenant.

Therefore, the covenant now stands, entirely one-sided: a covenant of promises that must be kept because the Father's side of it must stand, the other part of the covenant having been fulfilled by the Son. God cannot, and He will not, draw back from doing what He covenanted with Christ to do. The Lord Jesus will receive the joy that was set before Him (Hebrews 12:2).

> **This is now a covenant of pure grace; let no man attempt to mix works with it.**

"He shall see of the travail of his soul, and shall be satisfied: by his knowledge shall [Jesus Christ who became God's] *righteous servant justify many"* (Isaiah 53:11), for has He not borne their iniquities? How could those who have Christ as their Surety not be accepted?

Do you see why it is that the covenant, as we have read it, stands so absolutely without *if*s, *but*s, and *maybe*s, and runs only on *shall*s and *will*s? It is because the one side of it that did look uncertain was committed into the hands of Christ, who cannot fail or be discouraged (Isaiah 42:4). He has completed His part of it. Now it stands fast, and so it must stand forever and ever.

This is now a covenant of pure grace and nothing else but grace. Let no man attempt to mix works with it, or anything else of human merit. God saves now because He chooses to save. Over the head of us all, there comes a sound as of a martial trumpet, and yet with a deep, inner, peaceful music to it: *"I will have mercy on whom I will have mercy, and I will have compassion on whom I will have compassion"* (Romans 9:15). God observes us, all lost and ruined, and in His infinite mercy comes with absolute promises of grace to those whom He has given to His Son Jesus.

So, that is the doctrine of the covenant.

Are You Included in the Covenant?

Now comes the important question, Are you personally included in this covenant? May the Holy Spirit help each of us to ascertain the truth on this point. I would earnestly urge you who are really anxious in heart to know the answer to read the epistle to the Galatians. Read that book through if you want to know whether you have any part or lot in the covenant of grace.

Perhaps you are asking, "Did Christ fulfill the law for me? Are the promises of God absolutely and unconditionally made to me?" You can know by answering the following three questions.

In Christ

The first question is, Are you in Christ? Did you notice that we were all in Adam, and in Adam we all fell? Now, *"as by one man's disobedience many were made sinners, so by the obedience of one shall many be made righteous"* (Romans 5:19). Are you in the Second Adam? You certainly were in the first one, for so you fell. Are you in the Second? Because, if you are in Him, you are saved in Him. He has kept the law for you.

The covenant of grace made with Christ was made with you if you are in Him. As surely as the sons of Levi were in the loins of Abraham when Melchizedek met him (see Hebrews 7:1, 5), so were all believers in the loins of Christ when He died upon the cross. If you are in Christ, you are a part of the Seed to whom the promise was made. However, there is only one Seed, as the apostle Paul said, *"He saith not, And to seeds, as of many; but as of one, And to thy seed, which is Christ"* (Galatians 3:16). If, then, you are in Christ, you are in the Seed, and the covenant of grace was made with you.

Faith in Jesus

The second question is, Do you have faith? By ascertaining your response to this question you will be helped to answer the previous one, because believers are in Christ. In the epistle to the Galatians, you will find that the mark of those who are in Christ is their belief in Christ. The mark of all who are saved is not confidence in works, but faith in Christ. In writing Galatians, Paul insisted upon it: *"But that no man is justified by the law in the sight of God, it is evident: for, The just shall live by faith"* (Galatians 3:11), and the law is not of faith. Over and over again he stated it.

Come, then, do you believe in Jesus Christ with all your heart? Is He your sole hope for heaven? Do you lean your whole weight, the entire strength of your salvation, on Jesus? Then, you are in Him, and the covenant is yours. There is not one blessing God has decreed to give that He will not give to you. There is not a benefit that He has determined, out of the grandeur of His heart, to bestow on His elect, which He will not bestow upon you. You have the mark, the seal, the badge of His chosen if you believe in Christ Jesus.

Born Again

Another question that should help you is, Have you been born again? I refer you again to Galatians, which I would like every anxious person to read through very carefully. You will see that Abraham had two sons. One of them, Ishmael, the child of the bondwoman, was born according to the flesh. Although he was the firstborn son, he was not the heir, for Sarah said to Abraham, *"Cast out the bondwoman and her son: for the son of the bondwoman shall not be heir with the son of the freewoman"* (Galatians 4:30). He who was born after the flesh did not inherit the covenant promise.

Is your hope of heaven fixed on the fact that you have a good mother and father? Then, your hope is born after the flesh, and you are not in the covenant. I constantly hear it said that children of godly parents do not need to be converted. Let me denounce that wicked falsehood. *"That which is born of the flesh is flesh"* (John 3:6), and nothing better. Those who are born after the flesh are not the children of God. Do not trust in gracious descent or in holy ancestors. *"Ye must be born again"* (John 3:7), every single one of you, or you will perish forever, whoever your parents may be.

Abraham had another son, Isaac, who was not born by the strength of his father, nor after the flesh at all, for we are told that both Abraham and Sarah had become old. Rather, Isaac was born by God's power, according to promise. He was the child given by grace. Now, have you ever been born like that— not by human strength but by power divine? Is the life that is in you a life given by God? The true life is not born of the will of man, nor of blood, nor of natural excellence (John 1:13). Instead, eternal life comes by the working of the Holy Spirit, and it is *"the gift of God...through Jesus Christ our Lord"* (Romans 6:23). If you have this life, you indeed are included in the covenant, for it is written,

> *Neither, because they are the seed of Abraham, are they all children: but, In Isaac shall thy seed be called. That is, they which are the children of the flesh, these are not the children of God: but the children of the promise are counted for the seed.* (Romans 9:7–8)

God said to Abraham, *"In thy seed shall all the nations of the earth be blessed"* (Genesis 22:18). That was because He meant to justify the Gentiles by faith, so that the blessing given to believing Abraham might come to all believers (Galatians 3:14). Abraham is often called the father of the faithful or *"the father of all them that believe"* (Romans 4:11). With such is the covenant established.

Blessed Assurance

Here, then, are the test questions:

- Am I in Christ?
- Do I have faith in Jesus?
- Am I born again by the Spirit of God according to the promise and not according to my works or to my fleshly birth?

If you can answer in the affirmative, then you are in the covenant and your name stands in the eternal record. Before the stars began to shine, the Lord had covenanted to bless you. Before evening and morning made the first day, your name was in His book. Before the world's foundation was laid, Christ shook hands with the Father in the council chamber of eternity and pledged Himself to redeem you and to bring you and multitudes of others into His eternal glory. Christ will do it, too, for He never breaks His guaranteed pledge any more than the Father breaks His covenant word.

I want you to be quite sure about these points, for what peace it will nurture in your soul, what a restfulness of heart it will be for you to understand the covenant and to know that your name is in it!

Are the Covenant Blessings for Me?

If indeed we can believe the good evidence of God's Word that we are of the Seed with whom the covenant was made in Christ Jesus, then every blessing of the covenant will come to us. I will put it in a little more personal terms: If you are of the covenanted Seed, every blessing of the covenant will come to you.

The devil says, "No, it won't." Why not, Satan? "Why," says he, "you are not able to do this or that." Refer the devil to our text, tell him to read those passages that we have read, and ask him if he can spy an *if* or a *but* in them. I cannot.

"But, but, but," Satan sputters, "you cannot do enough. You cannot feel enough." Does it say anything about feeling there? It only says, *"[I] will give them an heart of flesh"* (Ezekiel 11:19). They will feel enough then.

"But," the devil says, "you cannot soften your hard heart." Does it say that you are to do so? Does it not say *"I will take the stony heart out of their flesh"* (v. 19)? The whole tone of the passage is that God will do it, and therefore God will do it. The devil dares not say that God cannot do it, because he knows that God can even enable us to tread him under our feet (Luke 10:19).

Satan says, "You will never be able to keep on the right path if you become a Christian." Does it say anything about that in the covenant further than this: *"I will...cause you to walk in my statutes"* (Ezekiel 36:27)? What if we do not have the power in and of ourselves to continue in God's statutes? God has the power to make us continue in them. He can work obedience and final perseverance in holiness in us; His covenant promises these blessings to us.

Wholly the Gift of God

To come back to what we said before, God does not ask of us, but He gives to us. He sees us dead in trespasses and sins, and He loves us even when we are so. He sees us feeble, unable to help ourselves, yet He comes in and works in us *"to will and to do of his good pleasure"* (Philippians 2:13). Only then can we *"work out* [our] *own salvation with fear and trembling"* (Philippians 2:12).

> If you are of the covenanted Seed, every blessing of the covenant will come to you.

The bottom of it, the very foundation of it, is Christ Himself, and He finds nothing in us to help Him. There is neither fire nor wood in us, much less the lamb for the burnt offering, but all is emptiness and condemnation. He comes in with "I will do" and "you shall be," like a royal Helper affording free aid to destitute, helpless sinners, according to the riches of His grace. Now be assured that, having made such a covenant as this, God *"will ever be mindful"* of it.

Grace

God Gave His Word

He will do so, first, because He cannot lie. If He says He will, He will. His very name is *"God, that cannot lie"* (Titus 1:2). If I am a believer in Christ, I must be saved; nothing can prevent it. If I am a believer in Christ, I must be saved; all the devils in hell cannot stop it, for God has said, *"He that believeth on him is not condemned"* (John 3:18). *"He that believeth and is baptized shall be saved"* (Mark 16:16).

God's word is not first "yes" and then "no": *"For all the promises of God in him are yea, and in him Amen, unto the glory of God by us"* (2 Corinthians 1:20). He knew what He said when He spoke the covenant. He has never changed it, nor has He contradicted it.

Promised to You Through Christ

If, then, you are a believer, you must be saved, because you are in Christ to whom the promise is made. If you have the new life within, you must be saved, for hasn't this spiritual life been born again of the living and incorruptible Seed that lives and abides forever (1 Peter 1:23)?

Jesus said, *"The water that I shall give him shall be in him a well of water springing up into everlasting life"* (John 4:14). You have drunk the water Christ gave you; therefore, it must spring up into everlasting life. It is not possible for death to kill the life that God has given you, nor for all the fallen spirits to tread out the divine fire that Christ's own Spirit has cast into your bosom. You must be saved, for God *"cannot deny himself"* (2 Timothy 2:13).

Freely Made

Next, God made the covenant freely. If He had not meant to keep it, He would not have made it.

When a man is driven into a corner by someone who says, "You must pay me now," the debtor is apt to promise more than he can perform. He solemnly declares, "I will pay you in two weeks." Poor fellow, he has no money now and will not have any then, but he made a promise because he could not help himself.

No such necessity can be imagined with God Almighty. The Lord was under no compulsion whatsoever. He could have left men to perish because of sin. There was no one to prompt Him to make the covenant of grace or even to suggest the idea.

> *Who hath directed the Spirit of the LORD, or being his counsellor hath taught him? With whom took he counsel, and who instructed him, and taught him in the path of judgment, and taught him knowledge, and showed to him the way of understanding?* (Isaiah 40:13–14)

He made the covenant of His own royal will. Be assured that, having made it, God will never turn back from it. A covenant so freely made must be fully carried out.

Grace

Sealed in Blood

Moreover, on the covenant document is a seal. Did you see it? The grand thing in a deeded gift is the signature or seal. What is this, this red splash at the bottom of it? Is it blood? Yes, it is. Whose blood? It is the blood of the Son of God. This has ratified and sealed the covenant. Jesus' shed blood in His death has made the covenant sure. Can God forget the blood of His dear Son or show contempt for His sacrifice? Impossible. Christ will save all those for whom He died as a covenant substitute. The redeemed will not be left in captivity as if the ransom price had effected nothing. Has He not said, *"All that the Father giveth me shall come to me; and him that cometh to me I will in no wise cast out"* (John 6:37)? That covenant stands secure, though the earth pass away, because the Father can never reject Christ's shed blood.

> **A covenant so freely made, of His own royal will, must be fully carried out.**

God's Delight

God delights in the covenant, and so we are sure He will not turn back from it. It is the joy of His holy heart. He delights to do His people good. To pass over transgression, iniquity, and sin is the recreation of Jehovah. Did you ever hear of God singing? It is extraordinary that the Divine One would solace Himself with song, yet a prophet has thus revealed the Lord to us.

The Covenant of Grace

The LORD thy God in the midst of thee is mighty;
he will save, he will rejoice over thee with joy; he will
rest in his love, he will joy over thee with singing.
(Zephaniah 3:17)

The covenant is the heart of God written out in the blood of Jesus. Since the whole nature of God runs parallel with the tenor of the everlasting covenant, you may rest assured that even its tiniest points stand secure.

God's Solemn Oath

Finally, you who are in the covenant dare not doubt that God will save you, keep you, and bless you, assuming you have believed on Jesus, are in Jesus, and are quickened into newness of life! You will not doubt when I explain one more thing. If your father, your brother, or your dearest friend had solemnly stated a fact, would you allow anybody to say that he had lied? No, I know you would be indignant at such a charge. Now, suppose your father in his most solemn manner had taken an oath. Would you for a moment think that he had perjured himself and had sworn a lie? You would never for a moment think such a thing.

Now, turn to the book of Hebrews, and you will find that God, because He knew that an oath among men is the end of strife (Hebrews 6:16), was pleased to seal the covenant with His oath:

Wherein God, willing more abundantly to show unto the
heirs of promise the immutability of his counsel, con-
firmed it by an oath: that by two immutable things, in

*which it was impossible for God to lie, we might have a
strong consolation, who have fled for refuge to lay hold
upon the hope set before us.* (Hebrews 6:17–18)

God has raised His hand and sworn that Christ
will have the reward of His passion; that His purchased
ones will be brought under His sovereign power; that
having borne sin and put it away, it will never be a
second time charged against His redeemed. His oath is
unbreakable.

This is all of it. Do you believe in Christ? Then,
God will work in you *"to will and to do of his good pleasure"*
(Philippians 2:13). God will conquer your sin; God will
sanctify you; God will save you; God will keep you;
God will bring you to Himself. Rest in the covenant.
Then, moved by intense gratitude, go forward to serve
your Lord with all your heart and soul and strength.
Being saved, live to praise Him. Do not work so
that you may be saved, but serve Him because you
are saved, for the covenant has secured your safety.
Delivered from the servile fear that an Ishmael might
have known, live the joyous life of an Isaac. Moved by
love of the Father, spend and be spent for His sake. If
the selfish hope of winning heaven by works has moved
some men to great sacrifice, so much more should the
godly motive of gratitude to Him, who has done all this
for us, move us to the noblest service and make us feel
that it is not a sacrifice at all.

*For the love of Christ constraineth us; because we thus
judge, that if one died for all, then were all dead: and*

The Covenant of Grace

*that he died for all, that they which live should not
henceforth live unto themselves, but unto him which
died for them, and rose again.*

(2 Corinthians 5:14–15)

*Know ye not that...ye are not your own? For ye are
bought with a price.*   (1 Corinthians 6:19–20)

If you are saved under the covenant of grace, the
mark of the covenanted ones is upon you, and the
sacred character of the covenanted ones should be dis-
played in you. Bless and magnify your covenant God.
Take the cup of the covenant, and call upon His name.
Plead the promises of the covenant, and have whatever
you need.

Chapter Two

Salvation Altogether by Grace

Two
Salvation Altogether by Grace

[God], who hath saved us, and called us with an holy calling, not according to our works, but according to his own purpose and grace, which was given us in Christ Jesus before the world began.
—2 Timothy 1:9

To influence persons of thought, we must use solid reasoning. Shallow minds may be impressed by mere warmth of emotion and force of excitement, but the more intellectual part of the community must be dealt with in quite another manner. When the apostle Paul desired to influence Timothy, his son in the faith, who was a diligent and earnest student and a man of gifts as well as of grace, he did not attempt to persuade him by mere appeals to his feelings. Instead, Paul felt that the most effective way to appeal to him was to remind him of solid doctrinal truth, which he knew Timothy believed.

Salvation Altogether by Grace

The ministry at large needs to heed this lesson. Certain earnest preachers are incessantly exciting the people but seldom, if ever, instructing them. They carry much fire and very little light. God forbid that we should say a word against appealing to the feelings—this is definitely needed in its place—but there is a balance to be observed with it. A religion that is based upon, sustained, and maintained simply by excitement will necessarily be flimsy and insubstantial and will yield very speedily to the crush of opposition or to the crumbling hand of time. The preacher may touch the feelings by rousing appeals, just as the harpist touches the harpstrings. He would be very foolish if he neglected such an admirable instrument. Still, as he is dealing with reasonable creatures, he must not forget to enlighten the intellect and instruct the understanding.

> **Preachers who merely excite but don't instruct carry much fire but little light.**

How can an evangelist appeal to the understanding better than by presenting the truth that the Holy Spirit teaches? Scriptural doctrine must furnish us with powerful motives to urge upon the minds of Christians. It seems to me that if I could, by some unreasoning impulse, move you to a certain course of action, it might be good in its own way for the immediate gain. However, in the long run, it would prove to be unsafe and untrustworthy, because you would be equally open to be moved in an opposite direction by other persons more skillful in such operations. Only when God enables us by His Spirit to influence our minds by solid truth and arguments of substance will we then move with a constancy of power that nothing can turn aside.

A feather floats on the wind, but it has no inherent power to move. Consequently, when the gale is over, it falls to the ground. Such is the religion of excitement. In contrast, the eagle has life within itself, and its wings bear it aloft and onward whether the breeze favors it or not. Such is religion when sustained by a conviction of the truth. The well-taught man in Christ Jesus stands firm where the uninstructed infant would fall or be carried away. *"Henceforth be no more children, tossed to and fro, and carried about with every wind of doctrine"* (Ephesians 4:14), wrote Paul. Those who are well established in the truth as it is in Jesus are least likely to be so carried away.

It is somewhat remarkable—at least it may seem so to people who are not accustomed to thinking about the subject—that Paul, in order to excite Timothy to boldness and to keep him constant in the faith, reminded him of the great doctrine that the grace of God reigns in the salvation of men. He gave in this verse—this parenthetical verse as some call it, but which seems to me to be fully in the flow of the passage—a brief summary of the Gospel, showing the great prominence that it gives to the grace of God. Paul did so with the design of maintaining Timothy in the boldness of his testimony for Christ.

Salvation Altogether by Grace

I do not doubt that a far greater power for usefulness lies concealed within the doctrines of grace than some men have ever dreamed of. It has been prevalent to look upon doctrinal truth as being nothing more than impractical theory, yet many have spoken of the ordinances of God's Word as being more practical and more useful. The day may come when in clearer light we will perceive that sound doctrine is the very root and vital energy of practical holiness and that to teach the people the truth that God has revealed is the readiest and surest way of leading them to obedience and persevering holiness.

May the Holy Spirit assist us as we consider, first, the doctrine taught in this text, and, second, the applications of that doctrine.

The Doctrine Explained

Readers, please remember that it is not my objective to extol doctrine that is the most popular or most palatable, nor do I desire to set forth the views of any one individual. My one aim is to give what I judge to be the meaning of the text. I probably deliver doctrinal principles that many of you may not like. Truly, I would not be at all surprised if you did not like it. Even if you become vexed and angry, I will not be at all alarmed, because I have never believed that I was commissioned to teach what would please my readers or that I was expected by sensible and gracious people to shape my views to suit the notions of my audience. I count myself responsive to God and to the text. If I explain the meaning of the text, I believe that I will give the mind of God and will be likely to have His favor, which will be sufficient for me—whoever may contradict me. However, let every candid mind be willing to receive the truth if what I am expressing is clearly in the inspired Word.

The Author of Salvation

In stating his doctrine in the following words, "[God], *who hath saved us, and called us with an holy calling, not according to our works, but according to his own purpose and grace, which was given us in Christ Jesus before the world began,*" the apostle Paul declared God to be the Author of salvation, "*who hath saved us, and called us.*" The whole tenor of the verse is directed toward a strong affirmation of Jonah's doctrine: "*Salvation is of the LORD*" (Jonah 2:9). To rationalize salvation by man from this text would require a very great twisting, involving more than ingenuity—indeed, it would require out-and-out dishonesty. But, to find salvation altogether from God in this verse is to perceive the truth that lies at the very surface. There is no need for profound inquiry into such an evident truth. "*Wayfaring men, though fools, shall not err therein*" (Isaiah 35:8).

> **Sound doctrine is the very root and vital energy of practical holiness.**

The text says as plainly as any words can say that God "*hath saved us, and called us with an holy calling.*" The apostle Paul, then, in order to bring forth the truth that salvation is through grace, declared that it is by God, that it springs directly and entirely from Him, and that it is from Him only. Is this not according to the teaching of the Holy Spirit in other places, where He affirms repeatedly that the Alpha and Omega of our salvation must be found not in ourselves but in our God?

In saying that God has saved us, Paul was referring to all the persons of the divine Trinity. The Father has saved us. *"God hath given to us eternal life"* (1 John 5:11). *"The Father himself loveth you"* (John 16:27). It was He whose gracious mind first conceived the thought of redeeming His chosen from the ruin of the Fall. It was His mind that first planned the way of salvation by substitution. From His generous heart the thought first sprang that Christ should suffer as the Covenant Head of His people, as the apostle Paul said:

> *Blessed be the God and Father of our Lord Jesus Christ, who hath blessed us with all spiritual blessings in heavenly places in Christ: according as he hath chosen us in him before the foundation of the world, that we should be holy and without blame before him in love: having predestinated us unto the adoption of children by Jesus Christ to himself, according to the good pleasure of his will, to the praise of the glory of his grace, wherein he hath made us accepted in the beloved.* (Ephesians 1:3–6)

From the depths of divine compassion came the gift of the only begotten Son: *"For God so loved the world, that he gave his only begotten Son, that whosoever believeth in him*

Grace

should not perish, but have everlasting life" (John 3:16). The Father selected the people who would receive an interest in the redemption of His Son, for these are described as *"called according to his purpose"* (Romans 8:28). The plan of salvation in all its details came forth from the Father's wisdom and grace.

The apostle Paul did not, however, overlook the work of the Son. It is most certainly through the Son of God that we are saved, for is not His name Jesus, the Savior? Incarnate in the flesh, His holy life is the righteousness in which saints are arrayed, while His igno-minious and painful death has filled the sacred bath of blood in which the sinner must be washed so that he may be

> **The Alpha and Omega of our salvation is found in God, not in ourselves.**

made clean. Through the redemption that is in Christ Jesus, the people of God become *"accepted in the beloved"* (Ephesians 1:6). With one voice before the eternal throne, they sing, *"Unto him that loved us, and washed us from our sins in his own blood...to him be glory"* (Revelation 1:5–6). They chant that hymn because He deserves the glory that they ascribe to Him. It is the Son of God who is the Savior of men; men are not the saviors of themselves.

Nor did the apostle Paul, I am persuaded, forget the third person in the blessed Trinity, the Holy Spirit. Who but the Holy Spirit first gives us power to under-stand the Gospel?

Salvation Altogether by Grace

Now we have received, not the spirit of the world, but the spirit which is of God; that we might know the things that are freely given to us of God...But the natural man receiveth not the things of the Spirit of God: for they are foolishness unto him: neither can he know them, because they are spiritually discerned.

(1 Corinthians 2:12, 14)

Does not the Holy Spirit influence our will, turning us from the obstinacy of our former rebellion to the obedience of the truth? Does not the Holy Spirit renew us, creating us *"in Christ Jesus unto good works"* (Ephesians 2:10)? Is it not by the Holy Spirit's breath that we live the spiritual life? Is He not to us Instructor, Comforter, and Quickener; is He not everything, in fact, through His active operations upon our minds?

Thus, the Father in planning, the Son in redeeming, and the Spirit in applying the redemption must be spoken of as the one God *"who hath saved us."*

Beloved, to say that we save ourselves is to utter a manifest absurdity. In Scripture, each of us is called a *"temple of God"* (1 Corinthians 3:16), a holy temple of the Lord. However, will anyone assert that the stones of the edifice in which he now resides were their own architect? Would anyone dare say that the stones of the building in which he now abides cut themselves into their present shape, spontaneously came together, and then piled themselves up into a spacious edifice? Should someone assert such a foolish thing, we would be disposed to doubt his sanity. Much more may we suspect the spiritual sanity of any man who would venture to affirm that the great temple of the church, the body of Christ, designed and erected itself. No, we believe that God the Father was the Architect, who sketched the plan, supplied the materials, and will complete the work.

Will it also be said that those who are redeemed have redeemed themselves? Or, that slaves of Satan break their own chains? If that were true, then why was a Redeemer needed at all? Why would there be any need for Jesus to descend into the world to redeem those who could redeem themselves? Do you believe that the sheep of God, whom He has taken from between the jaws of the lion, could have rescued themselves? It would be a strange thing if such were the case. Our Lord Jesus did not come to do an unessential work. However, if He had come to save persons who might have saved themselves, He certainly came without a necessity for so doing. We cannot believe that Christ came to do what sinners might have done themselves. No, He said of Himself, *"I have trodden the winepress alone; and of the people there was none with me"* (Isaiah 63:3), and the redemption of His people will give glory unto Himself only.

Will it be asserted that those who were once dead spiritually have quickened themselves? Can the dead make themselves alive? Who will assert that Lazarus, rotting in the grave, came forth to life by himself?

Even if that is accepted, still we will not believe that the dead in sin have ever quickened themselves. Those who are saved by God the Holy Spirit are created anew according to Scripture, but who ever dreamed of creation creating itself? God spoke the world into existence out of nothing, but nothing did not aid in the creation of the universe. Divine energy can do everything, but what can nothing do?

"Therefore if any man be in Christ, he is a new creature: old things are passed away; behold, all things are become new" (2 Corinthians 5:17). If we have become new creations, there must have been a Creator. Further, it is clear that, having then been spiritually dead, we could not have assisted in our own new creation, unless, indeed, death can assist life and nonexistence can aid in creation. The carnal mind does not assist the Spirit

> **Our Lord Jesus did not come to do an unessential work; we cannot save ourselves.**

of God in creating a new man, but regeneration is altogether the work of the Holy Spirit. Thus, the work of renewal is from His unassisted power.

Father, Son, and Spirit we then adore. Putting these thoughts together, we humbly prostrate ourselves at the foot of the throne of the august Majesty and acknowledge that, if we are saved, He alone has saved us. Unto Him be all the glory.

God's Unique Method

Next, we find in this verse that grace becomes conspicuous when we see that God pursues a remarkable method: *"who hath saved us, and called us."* The singularity of the manner lies in three things, which we will examine in turn.

In Totality

The first characteristic of God's method is the completeness of it. The apostle used the perfect tense when he wrote, *"who hath saved us."* Believers in Christ Jesus are saved. They are not looked upon as persons who are in a hopeful state and may ultimately be saved, but they are already saved. This is not according to the common talk of some believers, for many of them speak of being saved when they come to die. However, it is according to the usage of Scripture to speak of us who are saved. Be it known right now that at this present moment every man and woman is either saved or lost. Salvation is not a blessing just to be enjoyed upon the deathbed and to be sung of in a future state above, but a matter to be obtained, received, promised, and enjoyed now.

God has saved His saints—not partly saved them, but perfectly and completely saved them. The Christian is perfectly saved in God's purpose. God has ordained him unto salvation, and that purpose is complete.

The Christian is also saved as to the price that has been paid for him, for this is done, not in part, but in whole. The substitutionary work that Christ has offered is not a certain proportion of the work to be done. *"It is finished"* (John 19:30) was the cry of the Savior before He died, and so it is complete.

Salvation Altogether by Grace

The believer is also perfectly saved in his Covenant Head. Just as we were utterly lost as soon as Adam fell, before we had committed any actual sin, so also every man in Christ was saved in the Second Adam when He finished His work. The Savior completed His work, and He did so in the sense in which Paul used that expression, *"who hath saved us."*

Singular Order

This completeness is one facet of God's method, but we must move on to the next. I want you to notice the order as well as the completeness in our text: *"who hath saved us, and called us."* What? He saved us before He called us? Yes, so the text says. But, is a man saved before he is called by grace? Not in his own experience, not as far as the work of God the Holy Spirit goes, but he is saved in God the Father's purpose, in God the Son's redemptive payment, and in the person's relationship to his Covenant Head. Moreover, he is saved in this respect: The work of his salvation has been completed, and he has only to receive it as a finished work.

In past times, when men were imprisoned for debts they could not pay, it would have been quite correct for you to step into the cell of a debtor and say to him, "I have freed you," if you had paid his debts and obtained an order for his discharge. He was still in prison at that moment, but you had really liberated him as soon as you paid his debts. It is true he was still in prison when you visited him, but he was not legally there. No sooner did he know that the debt had been paid and the receipt pleaded before proper authorities than the man obtained his liberty.

Likewise, the Lord Jesus Christ paid the incalculable debts of His people before they knew anything about it. Did He not pay them on the cross almost two thousand years ago to the utmost penny? Is this not the reason why, as soon as He meets with us in grace, He cries, "I have saved you. I have paid your debt. Take hold of the eternal life I am offering to you." We are, then, virtually, though not actually, saved before we are called. *"Who hath saved us, and called us."*

> **Salvation is not a blessing for just the deathbed; it is to be received and enjoyed now.**

With a Holy Calling

There is yet a third characteristic, and that is in connection with our holy calling. God has *"called us with an holy calling."* Those whom the Savior saved upon the tree are in due time effectively called to holiness by the power of God the Holy Spirit. They leave their sins; they endeavor to be like Christ; they choose holiness, not out of any compulsion, but from the influence of a new nature. This leads them to rejoice in holiness, just as naturally as they had before delighted in sin. The old nature loved everything that was evil, but the new nature cannot sin because it is *"born of God"* (1 John 3:9) and loves everything that is good.

Salvation Altogether by Grace

Did Paul mention this result of our calling in order to address those who say that God calls His people because He foresees their holiness? No, God calls them to that holiness (1 Thessalonians 4:7). That holiness is not a cause, but an effect. It is not the motive of His purpose, but the result of His purpose. He neither chose them nor called them because they were holy, but He called them so that they might be holy. Holiness is the beauty produced by His workmanship in them (Ephesians 2:10). The excellence that we see in a believer is as much the work of God as is the atonement itself.

Altogether by Grace

This second point brings out very sweetly the fullness of the grace of God. First, salvation must be of grace, because the Lord is the Author of it. What motive but grace could move Him to save the guilty? In the next place, salvation must be of grace because the Lord works in such a manner that *our* righteousness is forever excluded. Salvation is completed by God. Therefore, it is not of man, neither is it by man. Salvation is generated by God in an order that puts our holiness as a consequence and not as a cause. Thus, merit is forever disowned.

Not by Our Works

When a speaker desires to strengthen his point and to make himself clear, he generally includes a negative for contrast. Thus, the apostle Paul added a negative:

"not according to our works." The world's preaching is, "Do as well as you can, live a moral life, and God will save you." The gospel preaching is this: "You are a lost sinner and deserve nothing from God but His displeasure; if you are to be saved, it must be by an act of sovereign grace. God must freely extend the silver scepter of His love to you, for you are a guilty wretch who deserves to be sent to the lowest hell. Your best works are so full of sin that they can in no way save you. To the free mercy of God you owe all."

"Oh," someone says, "are good works of no use?" God's works are of use when a man is saved. They are the evidence of his being saved, but good works do not save a man. Good works do not influence the mind of God to save a man. If it were so, salvation would be a matter of debt and not of grace. The Lord has declared repeatedly in His Word, *"Not of works, lest any man should boast"* (Ephesians 2:9).

In his epistle to the Galatians, Paul was very strong about this point. Indeed, he thundered it out again and again and again. Paul denied that salvation is even so much as in part due to our works:

> *Knowing that a man is not justified by the works of the law, but by the faith of Jesus Christ, even we have believed in Jesus Christ, that we might be justified by the faith of Christ, and not by the works of the law: for by the works of the law shall no flesh be justified.* (Galatians 2:16)

Paul assured us that the two principles of grace and merit can no more mix together than fire and water; that if man is to be saved by the mercy of God, it must be by the mercy of God and not by works; and that if man is to be saved by works, it must be by works entirely and not by mercy mixed in, for mercy and works will not blend together.

> *And if by grace, then is it no more of works: otherwise grace is no more grace. But if it be of works, then is it no more grace: otherwise work is no more work.*
>
> (Romans 11:6)

Jesus saves, but He does all the work or none. He is Author and Finisher, and works must not rob Him of His due. Sinner, you must either receive salvation freely from the hand of Divine Bounty, or else you must earn it by your own unassisted merits, the latter being utterly impossible for any human being. Oh, may you yield to the first.

Good works do not save a man but are simply evidences of his being saved.

Friends, this is the truth that still needs to be preached. This is the truth that shook all of Europe from end to end when Luther first proclaimed it. Is this not one of the thunderbolts that the great Reformer hurled at Rome: *"Being justified freely by his grace through the redemption that is in Christ Jesus"* (Romans 3:24)?

But why did God make salvation to be by faith? Scripture tells us, *"Therefore it is of faith, that it might be by grace"* (Romans 4:16). If it had been by works, it must have been from debt; but since it is of faith, we can clearly see that there can be no deserving work in faith. It must be therefore by grace.

His Eternal Purpose

The text becomes even more explicit, for we find that God's eternal purpose is now mentioned. The next thing the apostle Paul said was this: *"Who hath saved us, and called us with an holy calling, not according to our works, but according to his own purpose."* Mark those words, *"according to his own purpose."* Oh, how some people squirm over those words, as if they were worms on a fisherman's hook! Yet, there it stands, and it cannot be eradicated. God saves His people "according to their purpose"— no, *"according to his own purpose."* My brothers and sisters, do you not see how all the merit and the power of the creature are eliminated when you are saved, not according to your purpose or merit but *"according to his own purpose"*?

I will not dwell on this, because it is not exactly the object of this study to bring out in full the great mystery of electing love, but I will not for a moment keep back the truth. If any man is saved, it is not because he purposed to be saved, but because God purposed to save him. Have you never read the Holy Spirit's testimony: *"It is not of him that willeth, nor of him that runneth, but of God that showeth mercy"* (Romans 9:16)?

The Savior said to His disciples what He in effect says also to us: *"Ye have not chosen me, but I have chosen you,*

Salvation Altogether by Grace

and ordained you, that ye should go and bring forth fruit" (John 15:16). Some people have one viewpoint and some hold another concerning the freedom of the will, but our Savior's statement was this: *"Ye will not come to me, that ye might have life"* (John 5:40). You will not come by your own will, because your will would never bring you. If you do come, it is only because you are so inclined by grace: *"No man can come to me, except the Father which hath sent me draw him"* (John 6:44). The person *"that cometh to me I will in no wise cast out"* (John 6:37) is a great and precious general Scripture, but it is quite consistent with the rest of the same verse: *"All that the Father giveth me shall come to me."*

Our text tells us that our salvation is *"according to his own purpose."* It is a strange thing that men should be so angry about the purpose of God. We ourselves have a purpose. We permit our fellow creatures to have some will of their own, especially in giving away their own goods, but supposedly God is to be bound and fettered by men and not permitted to do as He wills with His own. However, be this known unto you, O men who reply against God (Romans 9:20): He pays no attention to your arguments, but He asks you, "Can I not do as I will with My own?"

> *And all the inhabitants of the earth are reputed as nothing: and he doeth according to his will in the army of heaven, and among the inhabitants of the earth: and none can stay his hand, or say unto him, What doest thou?* (Daniel 4:35)

Grace

Dependent on Grace Alone

Lest we should make any mistake, the text then adds, *"according to his own purpose and grace."* The purpose of God is not founded on any foreseen merit of ours, but upon His grace alone. It is grace, all grace, and nothing but grace from first to last.

> **If any man is saved, it is because God purposed to save him.**

Man stands shivering outside, a condemned criminal, and God, sitting upon the throne, sends the herald to tell him that He is willing to receive sinners and to pardon them. The sinner replies, "Well, I am willing to be pardoned if I am permitted to do something in order to earn pardon. If I can stand before the King and claim that I have done something to win His favor, I am quite willing to come."

However, the herald replies, "No, if you are pardoned, you must understand that it is entirely and wholly as an act of grace on God's part. He sees absolutely nothing good in you. He knows that there is nothing good in you. He is willing to take you just as you are— bad, wicked, and undeserving. He is willing to give you graciously what He would not sell to you for any price (Isaiah 55:1) and what He knows you cannot earn from Him. Will you receive it?"

In the natural state, every man says, "No, the very idea is abhorrent to me. I will not be saved in that style." Well then, misguided soul, remember that you will never be saved at all, for God's way is salvation by grace. If ever you are saved, my dear one, you will have to confess that you never deserved or merited one single blessing from the God of grace. You will have to give all the glory to His holy name if you ever get to heaven.

Note that even in the matter of the acceptance of this offered mercy, you will never receive it unless He makes you willing. He does freely present it to every one of you, and He honestly bids you to come to Christ and live. However, I know that you will never come of your own accord, unless the effectual grace that first provided mercy makes you willing to accept that mercy by the working of the Holy Spirit. Thus, our text tells us it is *"according to his own purpose and grace."*

A Free Gift

Again, in order to shut out everything that might lead to boasting, the whole is spoken of as a gift. Do notice that. Lest we should still slip away from the fold—for we are such straying sheep in this matter—it is added, *"his own purpose and grace, which was given us."* The wording was not "which was sold to us," "which we earned," or "which was offered to us," but *"which was given us."* The apostle Paul stated it here in such a way that it would be a deathblow to all of our supposed merit: *"which was given us."* It was given to us. What can be freer than a gift, and what is more evidently of grace?

Grace

The Medium of Bestowal

Further, the gift is bestowed through a medium that glorified Christ. It is written, *"which was given us in Christ Jesus."* We ask to have mercy from the fountain-head of grace, but we dare not ask even to make the bucket in which the precious draught of grace is to be brought to us. Christ is to be the sacred vessel in which the grace of God is to be presented to our thirsty lips. Now, where is boasting? Why surely, there it sits at the foot of the cross and sings,

**God forbid that I should glory
Save in the cross of our Lord Jesus Christ.**

Is this not grace and grace alone? No room exists here for merit or works or boasting, but only for grateful, humble hearts to receive the *"grace, which was given us in Christ Jesus."*

From Eternity Past

Still further, a time frame is given in the text: *"before the world began."* These last words seem to me forever to lay prostrate all idea about anything of our own merits in saving ourselves, because it is here witnessed that God gave us grace *"before the world began."* Where were you then? What hand held you in it *"before the world began"*?

If you can, go back in your imagination to those ancient years when the venerable mountains were not yet formed, when world and sun and moon and stars were yet housed in God's great mind, when the unnavigated sea of space had never been disturbed by wings of seraphim, when the awesome silence of eternity had never been startled by the song of cherubim—when God dwelt alone. If you can conceive that time before all time, that vast eternity, it was then that God extended His *"grace, which was given us in Christ Jesus."* What, O soul, did you have to do with that? Where were your merits then? Where were you yourself? You who *"are counted as the small dust of the balance"* (Isaiah 40:15), you insect of a day, where were you? See how Jehovah reigned, dispensing mercy as He would, and ordaining unto

> **Christ is the vessel in which God's grace is presented to our thirsty lips.**

eternal life without taking counsel of man or angel, for neither man nor angel then had an existence. So that it might be all of grace, He gave us grace *"before the world began."*

I have honestly explained the doctrine of the text, and nothing more. If such is not the meaning of our text, I do not know the meaning of it, and I cannot therefore tell you what it is, but I believe that I have given the natural and grammatical teaching of the verse. If you do not like the doctrine, I cannot help it. I did not write the text, and if I have to expound it, I must expound it as honestly as it is in my Master's Word. I pray that you may receive what He says, whatever you may do with what I say.

The Efficacy of the Doctrine

Now, I will try to show some of the effects of the doctrine of grace, which has been set in the storeroom of religious remnants by many. It is acknowledged to be true, for it is confessed in most creeds: It is in the Church of England articles, and it is in the confessions of all sorts of Protestant Christians, except those who are avowedly Arminian. Yet, how little is it ever preached or taught! It has been put among the relics of the past, considered to be a respectable sort of retired officer who is not expected to see any more active service. Now, I believe that it is not an antiquated officer in the Master's army, but rather that it is as full of force and vigor as ever. So, what is the purpose of it?

Boldness

First, it is clear from the context that grace has a tendency to embolden the man who receives it. Paul told Timothy, *"Be not thou therefore ashamed of the testimony of our Lord"* (2 Timothy 1:8). He then gave this as the motive and reason: How could a man be ashamed when he believes that God has given him grace in Christ Jesus before the world existed?

Suppose a man is very poor. "What does it matter?" says he. "Though I have but a little oil in my bottle and a little meal in my barrel, yet I have a lot and a portion in everlasting things. My name is not in Burke's *Peerage,* but it is in the book of God's election and was there before the world began." Such a man dares look the most proud of his fellows in the face.

This was the doctrine on which the brave old Ironsides fed—the men who, when they rode to battle with the war cry of "The Lord of Hosts!", made the cavaliers fly before them like chaff before the wind. There is no doctrine like it for putting a backbone into a man and making him feel that he is made for something better than to be trodden down like straw for the dunghill beneath a despot's heel. Sneer whoever will, the elect of God derive a nobility from the divine choice that no royal lineage can outshine.

Confident Belief

I pray that free grace would be preached more often, because it gives men something to believe with confidence. The great mass of professing Christians know nothing of doctrine. Their religion consists in going a certain number of times to a place of worship, but they have no care for truth one way or another. I write without any prejudice in this matter; however, in the course of my very extensive pastorate, I have talked with a large number of people who have been members of other churches for years. When I have asked them a few questions about doctrinal matters, it did not seem to me that they were in error. They were perfectly willing to believe almost anything that any earnest man might teach them, but they did not know anything. They had no minds of their own and no definite opinions. Our children who have learned *The Westminster Assembly's*

Grace

Confession of Faith know more about the doctrines of grace and the doctrines of the Bible than hundreds of grown-up people who attend a ministry that very eloquently teaches nothing.

It was observed by a very excellent critic not long ago that if you were to hear thirteen lectures on astronomy or geology, you might get a pretty good idea about the science and the theoretical position of the person who gave the lectures; however, if you were to hear thirteen hundred sermons from some ministers, you would not know anything at all about what they were preaching or what their doctrinal sentiments were. It ought not to be so.

The reason why Puseyism* spreads so and why all sorts of other errors have such a foothold is because our people as a whole do not know what they believe. In contrast, the doctrines of the Gospel, if they have been well received, give to a man something that he knows, something that he holds on to, something that will become dear to him, and something for which he would be prepared to die if the fires of persecution were again kindled.

Keeping Power

Even better is the fact that this doctrine not only gives a man something to hold on to, but it also holds the man. Let a man once have it etched in his heart

---

*A system of High Church principles set forth in a series of tracts by Oxford theologian, Edward Pusey.

that salvation is of God, not of man, and that God's grace, not human merit, is to be glorified, and you will never get that belief out of him. It is the rarest thing in all the world to hear of such a man ever becoming an apostate from his faith.

Other doctrine is slippery ground, like the slope of a mountain composed of loose earth and rolling stones, down which the traveler may slide long before he can even get a transient foothold. However, this doctrine is like a granite step upon the eternal pyramid of truth. Get your feet on this, and there is no fear of slipping as far as doctrinal standing is concerned. If we would have our churches well instructed and holding fast to the truth,

> **Grace is the battering ram that God uses to shake the gates of hell.**

we must bring out the grand old gospel doctrine of the eternal purpose of God in Christ Jesus before the world began. Oh, may the Holy Spirit write it on our hearts!

Moreover, friends, this doctrine overwhelms, as with an avalanche, all the claims of the priesthood. Let it be told to men that they are saved by God, and they say at once, "Then what is the need of the priest?" If they are told it is God's grace, they reply, "Then the priest does not need our money to buy Masses and absolutions," and down the priest goes at once.

Grace

Beloved, this is the battering ram that God uses to shake the gates of hell. How much more forcible this truth is than the pretty essays of many divines, which have no more power than bulrushes, no more light than smoking flax. Why do you suppose people met in the woods during times of persecution, assembled by the thousands outside the town of Antwerp and such places on the Continent, in jeopardy of their lives? Do you suppose they would ever have come together to hear the poor milk-and-water theology of this age, or to receive the lukewarm, insipid pabulum of our modern anti-Calvinists? Not they, my friends. They needed stronger meat and a more savory diet to attract them thus. Do you imagine that, when it was death to listen to the preacher, men, under the shadows of night and amid the wings of tempest, would then listen to philosophical essays or to mere moral precepts or to diluted, adulterated, soulless, theological suppositions? No, there is no energy in that kind of thing to draw men together when they fear for their lives.

But, what did bring them together in the dead of night amid the glare of lightning and the roll of thunder? What idea brought them together? Why, the doctrine of the grace of God, the doctrine of Jesus, the doctrine of His servants: Paul, Augustine, Luther, and Calvin. Something in the doctrine touches the heart of the Christian and gives him the kind of food that his soul loves—savory meat, suitable to his heaven-born appetite. To hear this, men braved death and defied the sword.

Salvation Altogether by Grace

If we are once again to see the gospel of works sent back to the place from where it came, it must be by declaring the doctrines of the grace of God. When these are declared and vindicated in every place, we will yet again make those who deny grace know that they cannot stand their ground for a moment. There is no room for these enemies of the true Gospel where men of God wield *the sword of the LORD, and of Gideon* (Judges 7:20) by preaching the doctrines of the grace of God.

Change of Focus

Beloved, let a man receive these truths, let them be written in his heart by the Holy Spirit, and they will make him look up. He will say, "God has saved me!" and he will walk with a constant eye toward God. He will not forget to see the hand of God in nature and in providence. He will, on the contrary, discern the Lord working in all places and will humbly adore Him. He will not give the glory due to the Most High to laws of nature or schemes of government, but he will have respect for the unseen Ruler. "What the Lord says to me, that will I do" is the believer's language. "What is His will, that will I follow; what is His Word, that will I believe; what is His promise, on that I will live." It is a blessed habit to teach a man to look up to God in all things.

At the same time, this doctrine makes a man look down upon himself. "Ah," says he, "I am nothing; there is nothing in me to merit esteem. I have no goodness of my own. If I am saved, I cannot praise myself. I cannot in any way honor myself. God has done it. God alone has done it." Nothing makes the man so humble, but nothing makes him so glad. Nothing lays him so low at the mercy seat, but nothing makes him so brave to look his fellowman in the face. It is a grand truth. I pray to God that all of you would know its mighty power!

Comfort

Lastly, this precious truth is full of comfort to the sinner, and that is why I love it. As it has been preached by some, it has been exaggerated and made into a source of dread. Why, there are some who preach the doctrine of election as though it were a line of sharp spikes to keep a sinner from coming to Christ, or as though it were a menacing battle-ax to be pushed into the breast of a coming sinner to keep him away from mercy. Now, it is not so.

> **Nothing but grace makes a man so humble and, at the same time, so glad.**

Sinner, whoever you may be, wherever you may be, your greatest comfort should be to know that salvation is by grace. Why, if it were by merit, what would become of you? Suppose that God saved men on account of their merits. Where, then, would you drunkards be? Where would you swearers be? You who have been unclean and unchaste, you whose hearts have cursed

God, and you who even now do not love Him, where would you be?

However, when salvation is all of grace, then all of your past life, however black and filthy it may be, need not keep you from coming to Jesus. Christ receives sinners. God has elected sinners. He has elected some of the blackest of sinners, so why not you? He receives everyone who comes to Him; He will not cast you out. (See John 6:37.) There have been some who have hated Him, insulted Him to His face, burned His servants alive, and persecuted Him through His members. Yet, as soon as they have cried, *"God be merciful to me a sinner"* (Luke 18:13), He has given them mercy at once. He will give it to you if you are led to seek it.

If I had to tell you that you were to work out your own salvation apart from His grace, it would be an impossible prospect for you. Instead, it comes to you in this way: Filthy, there is washing for you! Dead, there is life for you! Naked, there is raiment for you! All undone and ruined, here is complete salvation for you! O soul, may you have the grace given to you to grasp it, and then you and I together will sing the praises of the glory of divine grace.

Chapter Three

Grace, the One Way of Salvation

Three

Grace, the One Way of Salvation

But we believe that through the grace of the Lord Jesus Christ we shall be saved, even as they.

—Acts 15:11

Y ou who are familiar with Scripture will recall that these are the words of the apostle Peter. Paul and Barnabas had been preaching the Gospel among the Gentiles with great success, but *"certain of the sect of the Pharisees which believed"* (Acts 15:5) could not get rid of their old Jewish bigotry and legalism. They vehemently urged that the converted Gentiles ought to be circumcised or else they could not be saved. They made a great clamor over this, causing no small dissension and disputing (Acts 15:2). The children of the bondwoman mustered all their forces, while the champions of glorious liberty arrayed themselves for the battle.

Grace, the One Way of Salvation

Paul and Barnabas, those valiant soldiers of the Cross, stood out stoutly against the ritualistic brothers, telling them that the rite of circumcision did not belong to the Gentiles at all and ought not to be forced upon them. They would not yield their principles of freedom to the dictation of the Judaizers, but scorned to bow their necks to the yoke of bondage.

It was agreed to bring the matter up for decision at Jerusalem before the apostles and elders. When all the elders had assembled, there seems to have been a considerable dispute. During the midst of it, Peter, speaking with his usual boldness and clearness, declared that it would be wrong to put a heavy yoke upon the necks of the Gentiles, which neither that generation of Jews nor their fathers had been able to bear (Acts 15:10). He then concluded his address by saying, in effect, "Although these people are not circumcised and ought not to be, yet we believe that there is no difference between the Jew and the Gentile, and *through the grace of the Lord Jesus Christ we shall be saved, even as they.*'" In this, Peter was not to be blamed but to be greatly commended, for he spoke under the influence of the Spirit of God.

An Apostolic Confession of Faith

We will use our study text—*"We believe that through the grace of the Lord Jesus Christ we shall be saved, even as they"*—as concisely as we can for three important purposes. In the first place, we will look upon it as an apostolic confession of faith.

Notice it begins with, *"We believe."* Thus, we will call it the "Apostles' Creed," and we may rest assured that it has quite as clear a right to that title as the highly esteemed composition that is commonly called the "Nicene Creed" or "Apostles' Creed."

Here, we find that Peter was speaking for the rest, for he declared, *"We believe."* Well, Peter, what do you believe? We are all at attention. Peter's statement of faith was, *"We believe that through the grace of the Lord Jesus Christ we shall be saved, even as they."*

There is a great deal of talk in our day—foolish, vainglorious, idiotic, senseless talk—on the subject of apostolic succession. Some people think they have the direct line from the apostles running right to their feet, and others believe that those who make the greatest boast about it have the least claim to it.

There are clergymen who imagine that because they happen to be in a church that is in open alliance with the state government, they must necessarily be ministers of the church, of which Christ said, *"My kingdom is not of this world"* (John 18:36). Now, I think that their union with the state is, in itself, a conclusive reply to all such claims to apostolic succession.

Moreover, I find many fatal points of difference between the apostles and their professed successors.

Grace, the One Way of Salvation

When did Peter or Paul become state-paid ministers? In what state church did they enroll themselves? What tithes did they receive? What rates did they levy? What constraints did they make upon the Jews and the Gentiles? Were they rectors or vicars, chaplains or deans, canons or curates? Did they sit in the Roman House of Lords dressed in lawn sleeves? Were they titled Right Reverend Fathers in God? Were they appointed by the prime minister of the day? Did they put on gowns and read prayers out of a book? Did they christen children and call them regenerate, and did they bury wicked reprobates in sure and certain hope of a blessed resurrection?

As opposite as light is from darkness were those apostles from the men who pretend to be their divinely-appointed successors. When will men cease to thrust their arrogant presences into our faces? Only when common sense, to say nothing of the religion of our country, has rebuked their presumption.

Ritualism or Grace?

One thing is clear from this "Apostles' Creed" that we have before us: The apostles did not believe in ritualism. Peter—why, some make him out to be the head of the church! Do some not say that he was the first pope? I am sure that if Peter were here, he would grow very angry with them for slandering him so scandalously. In his first epistle, Peter expressly warned others against *"being lords over God's heritage"* (1 Peter 5:3), and you may be sure he did not fall into that sin himself.

Grace

When he was asked for his confession of faith, Peter stood up and declared that he believed in salvation *"through the grace of the Lord Jesus Christ"* alone. *"We believe."* O bold apostle, what do you believe? Now, we can still hear his statement. Did Peter say, "We believe in circumcision; we believe in regeneration by baptism; we believe in the sacramental efficacy of the Lord's Supper; we believe in pompous ceremonies; we believe in priests and altars and robes and rubrics and incense and the Mass"? Absolutely not! He did not utter a syllable concerning anything of the kind. He declared, *"We believe that through the grace of the Lord Jesus Christ we* [who have been circumcised] *shall be saved, even as they* [who have not been circumcised]."

> **The apostles' true successors are those who teach salvation by the unmerited favor and free mercy of God.**

Peter made very small account, it seems, of ceremonies in the matter of salvation. He took care that no iota of Sacramentarianism would mar his explicit confession of faith. He gloried in no rite and rested in no ordinance. Peter's entire testimony concerned the grace of the Lord Jesus Christ. He said nothing whatever about ordinances, ceremonies, apostolic gifts, or ecclesiastical unction—his theme was grace, and grace alone.

My beloved, the true successors of the apostles are those who teach you that you are saved through the unmerited favor and free mercy of God, those who agree with Peter in their testimony, *"We believe that through the grace of the Lord Jesus Christ we shall be saved."* These are the men who preach to you the Gospel of salvation through the blood and righteousness of Jesus.

However, the pretending ministers who boast about their priesthood preach *"another gospel: which is not another; but there be some that trouble you, and would pervert the gospel of Christ"* (Galatians 1:6–7). Upon their heads will be the blood of deluded souls. They profess to regenerate others, but they will perish themselves. They talk of sacramental grace but will receive eternal destruction. Woe unto them, for they are deceivers. May the Lord deliver this land from their superstitions.

Merit Versus Grace

Another thing is very clear here. The apostle did not believe in self-righteousness. The creed of the world is, "Do your best, and it will be all right with you." To question this maxim is treason against the pride of human nature that forever clings to salvation by its own merits. Every man is born a Pharisee. Confidence in the self and reliance on the self are bred in the bone—and will come out in the flesh.

"What," says a man, "do you not believe that if a man does his best, he will fare well in the next world? Why, surely you know that we must all live as well as we can, every man according to his own light; and if every man follows out his own conscience, as closely as possible, certainly it will be well with him here and in the world to come. How could you possibly believe otherwise?"

That is not what Peter said. Peter did not say, "We believe we will be saved like other people through doing our best." He did not even say, "We believe if we act according to our own light, God will accept that little light for what it was." No, the apostle struck out on quite another track and solemnly affirmed, *"We believe that through the grace of the Lord Jesus Christ we shall be saved,"* not through our good works, not through anything that we do, not by the merit of anything that we feel or that we perform or that we promise to perform, but by grace, that is to say, by the free favor of God.

Every man is born a Pharisee.

> **Perish each thought of human pride,**
> **Let God alone be magnified.**

We believe that if we are ever saved at all, we must be saved gratis; saved as the gratuitous act of a bountiful God; saved by a gift, not by wages; saved by God's love, not by our own doings or merits. This is the apostles' creed: Salvation is all of grace from first to last, and the channel of that grace is the Lord Jesus Christ, who loved and lived and died and rose again for our salvation.

Those who preach mere morality, or set up any way except that of trusting in the grace of God through Christ Jesus, preach another gospel. They will be accursed, even though they preach it with an angel's eloquence. (See Galatians 1:8–9.) When the Lord comes to discern between the righteous and the wicked, their work will be burned in the fire as wood, hay, and stubble. But those who preach salvation by grace through Jesus Christ will find that their work, like gold and silver and precious stones, will abide the fire, and great will be their reward. (See 1 Corinthians 3:10–15.)

The Question of Free Will

I think it is very clear, again, from the text, that the apostles did not believe in salvation by the natural force of free will. I fail to detect a trace of the glorification of free will here. Peter put it, *"We believe that...we shall be saved."* Through what? Through our own unbiased will? Through the volition of our own well-balanced nature? Not at all, but *"We believe that through the grace of the Lord Jesus Christ we shall be saved."*

> **We believe that if we are ever saved at all, we must be saved gratis.**

Peter took the crown off the head of man in all respects and gave all glory to the grace of God. He extolled God, the gracious Sovereign, who *"will have mercy on whom* [He] *will have mercy, and* [who] *will have compassion on whom* [He] *will have compassion"* (Romans 9:15). I wish I had a voice of thunder to proclaim in every street of London this glorious doctrine:

Grace

Here is the old Reformation doctrine. This is the doctrine that will shake the very gates of hell if it is but faithfully preached. Oh, for an army of witnesses to publish abroad the Gospel of grace in its sovereignty, omnipotence, and fullness. If you are ever to have comfort, believe me, dear one, you must receive the doctrine of salvation by free grace into your soul as the delight and solace of your heart, for it is the living truth of the living God. Not by ritualism, not by good works, not by our own unaided free will, but by the grace of God alone are we saved.

> Not for the works which we have done,
> Or shall hereafter do,
> Hath God decreed on sinful worms
> Salvation to bestow.
>
> The glory, Lord, from first to last,
> Is due to Thee alone:
> Aught to ourselves we dare not take,
> Or rob Thee of Thy crown.

Human Ruin

Were I now to divide this apostles' creed into small pieces and examine it in detail, it would be easy to show that many important truths are contained within it. Most evidently, it implies the doctrine of human

Grace, the One Way of Salvation

ruin. *"We believe that...we shall be saved."* That statement assuredly implies that all of us need to be saved. The apostle Peter was as sound in the faith concerning the total depravity of human nature as was the apostle Paul. Peter viewed man as a lost creature, needing to be saved by grace. He believed in those three great Rs that Rowland Hill used to talk about—ruin, redemption, and regeneration. He saw most clearly man's ruin, or he would not have been so explicit about man's salvation.

If Peter were here preaching to us, he would not tell us that man, though he is a little fallen, is still a noble creature, who needs only a little assistance to be able to right himself. From some pulpits that awful unctuousness has oozed, anointing corruption with the oil of hypocrisy, besmearing the abomination of our depravity with sickening flattery!

> **We must clearly see man's ruin before we can understand the necessity for his salvation.**

Peter would not give any sanction to such false prophets. No, he would faithfully testify that man is dead in sin; that life is a gift; and that man is lost, utterly fallen, and completely undone. He wrote about the former lusts of our ignorance (1 Peter 1:14), of our vain conversation received by tradition from our fathers (1 Peter 1:18), and of the corruption that is in the world through lust (2 Peter 1:4). In our present text, he declared that the best of men, men such as himself and the other apostles, had need of salvation.

Grace

Consequently, they must have been originally among the lost, heirs of wrath just as all other men are.

I am sure that he was a firm believer in what are called the doctrines of grace, as he was certainly in his own person an illustrious trophy and everlasting monument of grace.

What a ring there is in that word *grace*. Why, it does one good to speak it and to hear it; it is, indeed, a charming sound, harmonious to the ear. When one feels the power of it, it is enough to make the soul leap out of the body for joy.

> **Grace! how good, how cheap, how free,**
> **Grace, how easy to be found!**
> **Only let your misery**
> **In the Savior's blood be drowned!**

Grace, how it suits a sinner! How it cheers a poor forlorn wanderer from God! Peter was not in a fog about this; his witness was as clear as crystal, decisive as the sentence of a judge. He believed that salvation was of God's free favor and God's almighty power. He spoke out like a man, "We believe that we are saved by grace."

Christ's Atonement for Sins

Our apostle was also most decided and explicit concerning the Atonement. Can you see the Atonement in the text, sparkling like a jewel in a well-made ring? We are saved *"through the grace of the Lord Jesus Christ."*

Grace, the One Way of Salvation

What did the apostle mean but the grace that came streaming from those wounds when the Savior hung on the cross? What did he mean but the grace that is revealed to us in the bleeding Sufferer who took our sins and carried our sorrows, so that we might be delivered from wrath through Him? Oh, that all were as clear about the Atonement as Peter was!

Peter had seen his Master. No, even more, his Master had looked at him and broken his heart, and afterward Christ had bound it up and given him much grace. Peter was thus not content to state: "We believe that we shall be saved through grace." Rather, he was careful to word it: *"We believe that through the grace of the Lord Jesus Christ we shall be saved."*

Dear ones, never have any questions upon the vital point of redemption by the shed blood of Jesus Christ. This is a fundamental truth. He who is in darkness upon this subject has no light in him. What the sun is to the heavens, the doctrine of a vicarious satisfaction is to theology. Atonement is the brain and spinal cord of Christianity. Take away the cleansing blood, and what is left for the guilty? Deny the substitutionary work of Jesus, and you have denied all that is precious in the New Testament. Never let us endure one wavering, doubtful thought about this all-important truth.

Eternal Security

It seems to me, too, that without straining the text, I might easily prove that Peter believed in the doctrine of the final perseverance of the saints. They were not, in a certain sense, it seems, perfectly saved when he spoke, but he said, *"We believe that...we shall be saved."* But, Peter, could someone not fall away and perish? "No," Peter would reply. "We believe that through the grace of the Lord Jesus Christ we shall be saved." How positively he expressed it!

I do desire that you, dear friends, get a firm and intelligent hold of the doctrine of the safety of the believer, which is as clear as noonday in the Scriptures. On the whole, you have learned it and can defend it well, but all of you should *"be ready always to give an answer to every man that asketh you a reason of the hope that is in you"* (1 Peter 3:15).

One of my congregation was met by those who do not believe this doctrine. They said to him, "You will fall away; look at your own weakness and tendency to sin." He responded, "No, I know I would if I were left to myself, but then Christ has promised that He will never leave me or forsake me." Then, they questioned, "But, might you be a believer in Christ today, yet perish tomorrow?" The question was met with this reply: "Do not tell me that falsehood: God's saints will never perish, neither will any pluck them out of Jesus' hand. As for your doctrine of the final falling of the Lord's blood-bought ones, if that is the Gospel, go and keep it to yourselves. As for me, I would not go two

> **As the sun is to the heavens, vicarious satisfaction is to theology.**

inches to listen to it; there is nothing in it to lay hold of; it is a bone without marrow; there is no strength, no comfort for the soul in it!"

If I know when I trust Christ that He will save me at the last, then I have something to rest upon, something worth living for, but if it is all a mere *if* or *but* or *maybe* or *perhaps*, a little of myself and a little of Christ, I am in a poor state indeed. A gospel that proclaims an uncertain salvation is a miserable deception. Away with such a gospel; it is a dishonor to Christ, and it is a discredit to God's people. It neither came from the Scriptures of truth, nor does it bring glory to God.

Thus, I have tried to reveal to you the apostles' creed: *"We believe that through the grace of the Lord Jesus Christ we shall be saved, even as they."*

The Statement of a Moral Convert

Having used the text as the apostles' confession of faith, I will explain it as the statement of a convert who had lived a moral life.

Let me show you what I mean. Observe the way in which Peter handled the case. A company of Jews had assembled to discuss a certain matter, and some of them looked very wise and brought up certain suggestions that were rather significant. Their discussion went something like this: "Well, perhaps these Gentile dogs may be saved. Yes, Jesus Christ told us to go and preach the Gospel to every creature; therefore, He must have included these Gentile dogs. We do not like them, though, and must keep them as much under our rules and regulations as we can; we must compel them to be circumcised; we must have them brought under the full rigor of the law; we cannot excuse them from wearing the yoke of bondage."

After that, the apostle Peter got up to speak. These gentlemen expected him to affirm them by saying, "Why, these 'Gentile dogs,' as you call them, can be saved, even as you." Instead, he adopted quite a different tone. He turned the tables and said to them, "We believe that you may be saved, even as they."

> **A gospel that proclaims uncertain salvation is a miserable deception.**

A modern parallel would be if I located twenty people who had been very bad and wicked, who had plunged into the deepest sin, but God's grace had met with them and made them new creatures in Christ Jesus. Suppose I brought these people before a church meeting, and there were some of the members who said, "Well, yes, we believe that a drunkard may be saved, and a person who has been a harlot may, perhaps, be saved, too." But imagine, now, that I were to stand up and reply, "Now, my dear friends, I believe that you may be saved even as these." What a rebuke it would be! And that is precisely what Peter meant: "Do not raise the question about whether they can be saved—the question is whether you, who have raised such a question, will be saved. *'We believe that through the grace of the Lord Jesus Christ we shall be saved, even as they.'"* Thus, Peter seemed to take the objectors aback and to put the Gentile believers first, in order to cast out the bad, proud, wicked, devilish spirit of self-righteousness.

The Favor of Christian Heritage

Now, beloved, some of us were favored by Providence with the great privilege of having Christian parents, and consequently we never did know a great deal of the open sin into which others have fallen. Some of us never were inside a theater in our lives, never saw a play, and do not know what it is like. There are some reading this who, perhaps, never did frequent a tavern, do not know a lascivious song, and never uttered an oath. This is cause for great thankfulness, very great thankfulness indeed. But, you excellent moralists, mind that you do not say in your hearts, "We are quite sure to be saved," for you do not have any advantage over the outward transgressor before God so as to entitle you to be saved in any less humbling manner. If you ever are saved, you will have to be saved in the same way as those who have been permitted to plunge into the most outrageous sin.

Your being restrained from overt offenses is a favor for you to be grateful for but not a virtue for you to trust in. Ascribe it to God's providential goodness, but do not wrap it about you as though it were to be your

Grace

wedding garment. If you do, your self-righteousness will be more dangerous to you than some men's open sins are to them. You do not know how the Savior put it: *"The publicans and the harlots go into the kingdom of God before you"* (Matthew 21:31).

Only One Way for All

You moral people must be saved by the grace of our Lord Jesus Christ—*"saved, even as they,"* the outcasts, the wanderers. You will not, you cannot, be saved in any other way, and you will not be saved at all if you do not submit to this way. You will not be permitted to enter heaven, good as you think yourselves to be, unless you come down to the terms and conditions that sovereign grace has laid down, namely, that you should trust Christ, and be saved by grace, *"even as they."*

To prove to you, dear friends, that this must be the case, I will suppose that you have picked out twenty people who have been good, in a moral sense, from their youth up. Now, these people must be saved just the same as those other twenty that I have picked out, who have been as bad as bad can be from their earliest childhood. The reason why is because these amiable persons fell in Adam just as surely as the outcasts did. They are as fully partakers of the curse of the Fall as the profane and drunken, and they were born in sin and shaped in iniquity just as the dissolute and the dishonest were. There is no difference in the blood of humanity; it flows from one polluted source and is tainted in all its channels.

Grace, the One Way of Salvation

The depravity of human nature does not belong merely to those who are born in dirty back courts and alleys, but it is as certainly manifest in those of you who were born in the best parts of the city. You dwellers in Hyde Park are as altogether born in sin as the denizens of Seven Dials. The west side of town is as sensual as the east. The corruption of those born in the castle at Windsor is as deep as the depravity of workhouse children.

> **No matter how good you think yourself to be, you cannot enter heaven unless it is under the terms of sovereign grace.**

You of the gentry are born with hearts as bad and as black as the poorest of the poor. Sons of Christian parents, do not imagine, because you spring from a godly ancestry, that your nature is not polluted like the nature of others. In this respect, we are all alike: We are born in sin (Psalm 51:5), and alike are we *"dead in trespasses and sins...children of wrath, even as others"* (Ephesians 2:1, 3).

Remember, too, that although you may not have sinned openly, as others have done, yet in your hearts you have, and it is by your hearts that you will be judged. How often a man may commit adultery or incur the guilt of theft in his soul, while his hand lays idly by his side! Do you not know that a look may have in it the essence of an unclean act and that a thought may commit murder as well as a hand? God takes note of heart sin as well as hand sin. If you have been outwardly moral, I am thankful for it, and I ask you to be thankful for it, too; but do not trust in it for justification, seeing that you must be saved, even as the worst of criminals are saved, because in heart, if not in life, you have been as bad as they.

The Same Pardon for All

Moreover, the method of pardon is the same in all cases. If you moralists are to be washed, where must you find the purifying bath? I have never discovered a fountain with the capacity except this one:

There is a fountain filled with blood,
Drawn from Immanuel's veins.

That fountain is for the dying thief as much as for you, and for you as much as for him. There is a robe of righteousness that is to cover the best among the living who profess Christ; that same robe of righteousness covered Saul of Tarsus, the bloody persecutor. If you of unspotted outward character are ever to have a robe of righteousness, you must wear the same one as he wore. There cannot be another nor a better one.

You who are conscious of outward innocence, humble yourselves at the foot of the cross, and come to Jesus just as empty-handed, just as brokenhearted, as if you had been outwardly among the vilest of the vile, and *"through the grace of the Lord Jesus Christ* [you] *will be saved, even as they."* May the Holy Spirit bring you to this.

Grace, the One Way of Salvation

I do not know whether anybody reading this has ever fallen into such an unwise thought as I have known some entertain. I met with a case of this sort only the other day. A very excellent and amiable young woman, when converted to God, said to me, "You know, sir, I used almost to wish that I were one of those very bad sinners whom you so often speak to and invite to come to Jesus, because I thought then I should feel my need more. That was my difficulty: I could not feel my need." But, see, dear friends, we believe that through the grace of our Lord Jesus Christ, we who have not plunged into black sin shall be saved even as they who have done so. Do not make this a difficulty for yourselves.

Others take the opposite excuse: "I could trust Christ if I had been kept from sin." The fact is that you unbelieving souls will not trust Christ whichever way you have lived, for from some quarter or other, you will find cause for your doubting. But when the Holy Spirit gives you faith, you big sinners will trust Christ quite as readily as those who have not been great open offenders, and you who have been preserved from open sin will trust Him as joyfully as the great transgressors.

Come, you sick souls, come to my Master! Do not say, "We would come if we were worse." Do not say, "We would come if we were better," but come as you are; come just as you are. Oh! If you are a sinner, Christ invites you. If you are lost, remember Christ came to save the lost. Do not single out your case and make it to be different from others, but come to the foot of the cross. You are welcome!

Grace

Just as thou art, without one trace
Of love, or joy, or inward grace,
Or meetness for the heavenly place,
O guilty sinner, come!

Come, hither bring thy boding fears,
Thy aching heart, thy bursting tears;
'Tis mercy's voice salutes thine ears,
O trembling sinner, come.

"The Spirit and the Bride say, Come,"
Rejoicing saints re-echo, Come;
Who faints, who thirsts, who will, may come:
Thy Savior bids thee come.

A Converted Sinner's Confession

So far, I have illustrated that the text is the creed of an apostle and the statement of faith of a moral person upon conversion. But, our text would not be fairly treated if I did not use it as the confession of the great outward sinner when converted.

I will now address those who, before conversion, indulged in gross sin. Such were some of you. Glory be to God! You have been washed; you have been cleansed. My dear brothers and sisters, I can rejoice over you. More precious are you by far in my eyes than all the precious gems that kings delight to wear, because you are my eternal joy and crown of rejoicing (1 Thessalonians 2:19). You have experienced a divine change. You are not what you once were. You are new creatures in Christ Jesus (2 Corinthians 5:17).

Now, I will explain our text in terms that apply to you. *"We believe that through the grace of the Lord Jesus Christ we shall be saved, even as they."* What do we mean? Why, we believe that we will be saved, even as the best are saved. I will split that thought, as it were, into individual instances.

Earthly Poverty

In many churches in the back pew or off to the side sits a very poor believer. I am always glad to see such a person in my church. He probably had thought that his clothes were not good enough to come in, but I hope none of you will ever stay away from church because of your clothes. Attend services anyhow. The poor are always welcome; at least, I am glad to see them, even if others are not.

But indeed, my poor friend is in dire financial straits. He perhaps would not like anybody to see the room where he lives. Yet, my brother, do you expect to have a poor man's salvation? Do you expect that when you get to heaven, you will be placed in a distant corner as a pauper pensioner? Do you think that Jesus will only give you the crumbs that fall from His table? "Oh, no!" I think I hear you say. "Oh, no! I will leave my poverty when I get to glory."

Some of our friends are rich. They have an abundance of this world's goods. We rejoice to think that they have, and hope that they will have, grace to make a proper use of this mercy. Nevertheless, we poor people believe that *"We shall be saved, even as they."* We do not believe that our poverty will make any difference in our share in divine grace, but we know that we will be as much loved of God as the earthly rich are, as much blessed in our poverty as they are in their riches, and as much enabled by divine grace to glorify God in our sphere as they are in theirs. We do not envy them. On the contrary, we ask grace from God that we may feel that if we are poor in pocket, yet we are rich in faith, and *"shall be saved, even as they."*

Lack of Talent

Others of you are not so much poor in money as you are poor in useful talent. You come up to chapel and fill your seat, and that is about all you can do. You drop your weekly offering in the basket. When that is done, you have done all, or nearly all, in your power. You cannot preach; you could not conduct a prayer meeting; you have hardly courage enough to give away a tract. Well, my dear friend, you are one of the timid ones, one of the little Benjamins, of whom there are many.

Now, do you expect that the Lord Jesus Christ will give you a secondhand robe to wear at His wedding feast? When you sit at the banquet, do you think He will serve you from cold and inferior dishes? "Oh, no!" you say, "Some of our fellows have great talents, and we

Grace, the One Way of Salvation

are glad that they have. We rejoice in their talents, but we believe that *'we shall be saved, even as they.'* We do not think that there will be any difference made in the divine distribution of mercies because of our degree of ability."

Here on earth, very proper distinctions are made between rich and poor, and between those who are learned and those who are unlearned. However, we believe that there is no distinction in the matter of salvation: *"We shall be saved, even as they."*

Many of you would preach ten times better than I do if you could get your tongues loosened to say what you feel. What red-hot sermons you would preach, and how earnest you would be in their delivery! The sermon that you could not preach will be set down to your account, while perhaps that discourse of mine will be a failure because I may not have preached it as I should have done, with pure motives and a zealous spirit. God knows what you would do if you could, and He judges, not so much according to what you do, as according to your will to do it. He takes the will for the deed, and you *"shall be saved, even as they"* who proclaim the truth with the tongue of fire.

> **There is no distinction—rich or poor, learned or unlearned— in matters of salvation.**

Weak in the Faith

Most likely, some doubting person is reading this. Whenever you sing or pray, you probably seldom focus on the victorious celebration of our Lord, but generally you cry out words of contrition. Well, my dear friend, you are a weakling. You are Mr. Much-afraid or Mr. Little-faith. But, how is your heart? What are your prospects? Do you believe that you will be put off with a second-rate salvation, that you will be admitted by the back door into heaven instead of through the gate of pearl? "Oh, no!" you say, "I am the weakest lamb in Jesus' fold, but I believe that I *'shall be saved, even as they'*—that is, even as they who are the strongest in grace, most useful in labor, and most mighty in faith."

Shortly, dear friends, I will be crossing the channel. I will suppose that a good stiff wind may arise and that the vessel may be driven off her course and be in danger. I imagine that as I walk the deck, I see a poor girl on board. She is very weak and ill, quite a contrast to the strong, burly passenger who is standing beside her, enjoying the salt spray and the rough wind. Now, suppose a storm comes up. Who of these two is safer? Well, I cannot see any difference, because if the ship goes to the bottom, they will both go, and if the ship gets to the other side of the channel, they will both land in security. The safety is equal when the thing upon which they depend is the same.

Likewise, if the weakest Christian is in the boat of salvation—that is, if he trusts Christ—he is as safe as the strongest Christian. If Christ failed the frail one, He would fail the strong one, too. If the weakest Christian who believes in Jesus does not get to heaven, then Peter himself will not get there. I am sure of this:

Grace, the One Way of Salvation

If the smallest star that Christ ever kindled does not blaze in eternity, neither will the brightest one. If any of you who have given yourselves to Jesus would be cast away, this would prove that Jesus is not able to save; then all of us must be cast away, too. Oh, yes! *"We believe that...we shall be saved, even as they."*

I will suppose for a moment that there has been a work of grace in a prison—Cold Bath Fields, if you like. Out of all the inmates, perhaps six thorough villains have been redeemed and made new creatures by the grace of God. If they have understood the text, as they look in Scripture at the lives of half a dozen apostles—let us say Peter, James, John, Matthew, Mark, and Paul—they might exclaim, *"'We believe that through the grace of our Lord Jesus Christ we shall be saved, even as they,'* even as those apostles are."

> **The weakest Christian is as safe as the strongest Christian if they are both in the boat of salvation.**

Can you catch the idea and make it your own? When artists have drawn pictures of the apostles, they have often put halos around their heads, very like a brass pan or something of that kind, as if to signify that they were some particular and special saints. But in reality, there was no such halo there; the painter is far from the fact. Seriously and thoughtfully, we say that twelve souls picked from the scum of creation who look to Christ shall be saved, even as the twelve apostles are saved. Halo or no halo, they will join in the same hallelujah to God and the Lamb.

Let us select three holy women: the three Marys whom we read about in the Gospels—the Marys whom Jesus loved and who loved Jesus. These holy women, we believe, shall be saved. Now, suppose that I go to one of our refuges for the wayward and find three girls there who were once of evil fame. The grace of God has met with them, and they are now three weeping Magdalenes, penitent for sin. These three might say, humbly, but positively, *"'We believe that through the grace of the Lord Jesus Christ we* [three reclaimed harlots] *shall be saved, even as they,'* the three holy matrons who lived near Christ and were His delight." "Oh!" says one, "This is grace indeed! This is plain speech and wonderful doctrine, that God would make no distinction between one sinner and another when we come to Him through Christ."

Dear friend, if you have understood this very simple statement, go to Jesus at once with your soul. May God enable you to obtain complete salvation at this very moment. I do pray that you come in faith to the Cross. I pray that my Master's grace will compel you to enter into a state of full dependence upon Jesus, and so into a state of salvation. If you are now led to believe on the Lord Jesus Christ, no matter how black the past may have been, please know that *"the blood of Jesus Christ his Son cleanseth us from all sin"* (1 John 1:7).

Chapter Four

All of Grace

Four
All of Grace

For by grace are ye saved through faith; and that not of
yourselves: it is the gift of God.
—Ephesians 2:8

Of the things that I have written about over
the years, this is the sum. My theology, as
it pertains to salvation, is contained within
the circle of these words. I rejoice also to remember
that those of my family who were ministers of Christ
before me preached this doctrine and none other. My
father, who is still able to bear his personal testimony
for his Lord, knows no other doctrine, and neither did
his father before him.

I am led to remember this by the fact that a somewhat singular circumstance, recorded in my memory,
connects this text with my grandfather and myself. The
event occurred many years ago. It was announced that

All of Grace

I was going to preach in a certain country town in the eastern counties. I am not often late, for I feel that punctuality is one of those little virtues that may prevent great sins. But, I have no control over railway delays and breakdowns. Thus, I was considerably tardy when I reached the appointed place. Like sensible people, they had begun their worship and had proceeded as far as the sermon.

As I neared the chapel, I perceived that someone was in the pulpit preaching, and who should the preacher be but my dear, venerable grandfather? He saw me as I came in the door and made my way up the aisle. At once he said, "Here comes my grandson! He may preach the Gospel better than I can, but he cannot preach a better Gospel—can you, Charles?"

As I made my way through the throng, I answered, "You can preach better than I can. Do, I pray, go on." But, he would not agree to that.

He insisted that I must take the sermon, and so I did, continuing with the subject just where he left off. "There," said he, "I was preaching on *'For by grace are ye saved.'* I have been setting forth the source and fountainhead of salvation, and I am now showing them the channel of it, through faith. Now, you take it from there and go on."

I am so much at home with these glorious truths that I did not feel any difficulty in taking from my grandfather the thread of his message and joining my thread to it, so as to continue without a break. Our agreement in the things of God made it easy for us to be joint-preachers of the same topic. I went on with *"through faith,"* and then I proceeded to the next point, *"and that not of yourselves."*

Based on this essential phrase, I was explaining the weakness and inability of human nature and the certainty that salvation could not be of ourselves, when I had my coattail pulled, and my beloved grandfather took his turn again. When I spoke of our depraved human nature, the good old man said, "I know most about that, dear friends." So he took up the parable, and for the next five minutes set forth a solemn and humbling description of our lost estate, the depravity of our natures, and the spiritual death under which we were found.

When he had said his say in a very gracious manner, his grandson was allowed to go on again, to the dear old man's great delight, for now and then he would say in a gentle tone, "Good! Good!" Once he said, "Tell them that again, Charles," and, of course, I did tell them once again. It was a happy exercise for me to share in bearing witness to truths of such vital importance that are so deeply impressed upon my heart.

While selecting this text, I seemed to hear that dear voice, which has been so long lost to the earth, saying to me, "Tell them that again." I am not contradicting the testimony of forefathers who are now with

God. If my grandfather could return to earth, he would find me where he left me, steadfast in the faith and true to that form of doctrine *"which was once delivered unto the saints"* (Jude 1:3).

I expound on the doctrines of grace because I believe them to be true, because I see them in the Scriptures, because my experience endears them to me, and because I see the holy result of them in believers. I confess they are nonetheless dear to me because the new intellectual school despises them. I would never consider the fact that a doctrine was new as a recommendation for it. Those truths that have enlightened so many ages appear to me to be ordained to remain throughout eternity.

> **Never accept a doctrine merely for the fact that it is new.**

The doctrine that I preach to you is that of the Puritans. It is the doctrine of Calvin, the doctrine of Augustine, the doctrine of Paul, the doctrine of the Holy Spirit. *"The author and finisher of our faith"* (Hebrews 12:2) Himself taught blessed truth that well agreed with our text; the doctrine of grace is the substance of the testimony of Jesus.

A Present Salvation

I will handle the text briefly, by way of making a few statements. The first statement is clearly contained in the text: There is present salvation.

When Paul wrote this epistle, he declared, "You are saved," not "shall be," or "may be," but "are." He did not write, "partly saved," or "on the way to being saved," or "hopeful of salvation," but, *"By grace are ye saved."* Let us be as clear on this point as he was, and let us never rest until we know that we are saved. At this moment we are either saved or unsaved. That is clear. To which class do we belong? I hope that, by the witness of the Holy Spirit, we may be so assured of our safety as to sing, *"The LORD is my strength and song, and he is become my salvation"* (Exodus 15:2).

Upon this I will not linger, but I will pass on to note the next point.

Present Salvation Must Be by Grace

If we can say of any man or of any set of people, "You are saved," we must preface or follow it with the words, *"By grace."* There is no other present salvation except that which begins and ends with grace. Among those who dwell around us, we find many who are complete strangers to the doctrine of grace. These poor souls never dream of present salvation. Possibly they trust that they may be saved when they die; they half hope that, after years of watchful holiness, they may, perhaps, be saved at last. But, to be saved now, and to know that they are saved, is quite beyond them, and they believe it is presumptuous to think so.

All of Grace

There can be no present salvation unless it is upon this foundation: *"By grace are ye saved."* It is a very singular thing that no one has risen up to preach a present salvation by works. I suppose it would be too absurd. The works being unfinished, the salvation would be incomplete; or, the salvation being complete, the main motive of the legalist would be gone.

Salvation must be by grace. If man is lost by sin, how can he be saved except through the grace of God? If he has sinned, he is condemned; how could he, of himself, reverse that condemnation? Suppose that he should keep the law all the rest of his life; he will then only have done what he was always bound to have done, and he will still be an unprofitable servant (Luke 17:10). What is to become of the past?

> There is no other present salvation except that which begins and ends with grace.

How can old sins be blotted out? How can the old ruin be rebuilt? According to Scripture and according to common sense, salvation can only be through the free favor of God.

Salvation in the present tense must be by the free favor of God. People may contend for salvation by works, but you will not hear anyone support his own argument by saying, "I am myself saved by what I have done." Few men would dare to express such inordinate arrogance. Pride could hardly control its swelling with such extravagant boasting. No, if we are now saved, it must be by the free favor of God.

Grace

No one professes to be an example of the opposite view.

To be complete, salvation must be by free favor. When they come to die, saints never conclude their lives by hoping in their good works. Those who have lived the most holy and useful lives invariably look to free grace in their final moments. I have never stood by the bedside of a godly man who reposed any confidence whatever in his own prayers, repentance, or piety. I have heard eminently holy men on their deathbeds quoting the words, *"Christ Jesus came into the world to save sinners"* (1 Timothy 1:15). In fact, the nearer men come to heaven, and the more prepared they are for it, the simpler their trust is in the merit of the Lord Jesus, and the more intensely they abhor all trust in themselves.

If this is the case in our last moments, when the conflict is almost over, how much more ought we to feel it to be so while we are in the thick of the fight. If a man is completely saved in this present time of warfare, how can it be except by grace? While he has to mourn over sin that dwells in him, while he has to confess innumerable shortcomings and transgressions, while sin is mixed with all he does, how can he believe that he is completely saved except that it is by the free favor of God?

Paul spoke of this salvation as belonging to the Ephesians: *"By grace are ye saved."* The Ephesians had been given to curious arts and works of divination.

They had thus made a covenant with the powers of darkness. Now, if people such as these were saved, it must have been by grace alone. So is it with us also. Our original condition and character render it certain that, if saved at all, we must owe it to the free favor of God. I know it is so in my own case, and I believe the same principle holds true for the rest of believers.

This is clear enough, and so I advance to the next observation.

By Grace Through Faith

A present salvation must be by grace, and salvation by grace must be through faith. You cannot understand salvation by grace by any other means than through faith. This live coal from the altar needs the golden tongs of faith with which to carry it.

I suppose that it would have been possible, if God had so willed it, that salvation might have been through works and yet still by grace. If Adam had perfectly obeyed the law of God, he would only have done what he was bound to do. So, if God had rewarded him, the reward itself must have been according-

> **Saints never conclude their lives by hoping in good works, but only in grace.**

ing to grace, since the Creator owes nothing to the creature. This system would have been very difficult to work on a practical level, even though its objective was perfect. However, in our case it would not work at all. Salvation in our case means deliverance from guilt and ruin, and this could not have been secured by a measure of good works, since we are not in a condition to perform any.

Suppose I had to preach that you, as sinners, must do certain works, and then you would be saved. Further, suppose that you could perform them. Such a salvation would not then be seen to be all of grace; it would soon appear to be of debt. Apprehended in such a fashion, it would have come to you in some measure as the reward of work done, and its whole aspect would have been changed. Salvation by grace can only be gripped by the hand of faith. The attempt to lay hold of it by the performance of certain acts of law would cause the grace to evaporate.

> *Therefore it is of faith, that it might be by grace.*
> (Romans 4:16)

> *And if by grace, then is it no more of works: otherwise grace is no more grace. But if it be of works, then is it no more grace: otherwise work is no more work.*
> (Romans 11:6)

Some try to lay hold of salvation by grace through the use of ceremonies, but it will not do. You are christened, confirmed, and caused to receive "the holy sacrament" from priestly hands. Does this bring you salvation? I ask you, "Do you have salvation?" You dare not say "Yes." If you did claim salvation of a sort, yet I am sure it would not be in your minds salvation by grace, for those who are most addicted to the performance of outward rites are usually the last persons to enjoy any assurance of being saved by grace. They do not even think to look for such a thing. The more they multiply their rites and ceremonies, the more they quit the notion of grace, and the more they lose the true idea of salvation.

Again, you cannot lay hold of salvation by grace through your feelings. The hand of faith is constructed for the grasping of a present salvation by grace, but feeling is not adapted for that end. If you say, "I must feel that I am saved; I must feel so much sorrow and so much joy, or else I will not admit that I am saved," you will find that this method will not suffice. You might as well hope to see with your ears or taste with your eyes or hear with your nose as to believe by feeling: it is the wrong organ. After you have believed, you can enjoy salvation by feeling its heavenly influences, but to dream of getting a grasp of it by your own feelings is as foolish as to attempt to carry the sunlight in the palm of your hand or the breath of heaven between the lashes of your eyes. There is an essential absurdity in the whole affair.

Moreover, the evidence yielded by feeling is singularly fickle. When your feelings are peaceful and delightful, they are soon broken in upon and become restless and melancholy. The most fickle of elements, the most feeble of creatures, or the most contemptible of circumstances may sink or raise our spirits. Mature men come to think less and less of their present emotions as they reflect upon the little reliance that can be safely placed in them.

Faith receives the statement of God concerning His way of gracious pardon, and thus it brings salvation to the man believing it. In contrast, feeling—warming under passionate appeals, yielding itself deliriously to a hope that it dares not examine, whirling round and round in a sort of dervish dance of excitement that has become necessary for its own sustaining—is all astir like the troubled sea that cannot rest.

> **You can only lay hold of salvation by the hand of faith, not through feelings.**

From its boiling and raging, feeling is apt to drop to lukewarmness, despondency, despair, and all similar states. Feelings are a set of cloudy, windy phenomena that cannot be trusted in reference to the eternal truths of God.

Not of Ourselves

We now take this discussion a step further. The present salvation and the faith and the whole gracious work altogether are not of ourselves.

First of all, they are not deserved because of our prior performance. They are not the reward for former good endeavors. No unregenerate person has lived so well that God is bound to give him further grace and to bestow on him eternal life. Otherwise, it would be no longer of grace, but of debt. Salvation is given to us, not earned by us. Our first life is always a wandering away from God, and our new life of return to God is always a work of undeserved mercy, performed in those who greatly need, but never deserve, such gracious favor.

In the further sense, it is not of ourselves in that it is not out of our internal excellence. Salvation comes from above. It is never evolved from within. Can eternal life be evolved from the bare ribs of death? Some dare to tell us that faith in Christ and the new birth are only the development of good things that lay hidden in us by nature. But in this, like their father the devil, they speak of their own (John 8:44). Beloved, if an heir of wrath is left to develop on his own, he will become more and more fit for the place prepared for the devil and his angels! You may educate an unregenerate man to the highest degree, yet, he remains, and must forever remain, dead in sin unless a higher power comes in to save him from himself.

Grace brings into the heart an entirely foreign element. That element does not improve and perpetuate. It kills and then makes alive. There is no continuity between the state of nature and the state of grace: The one is darkness, and the other is light; the one is death, and the other is life. Grace, when it comes to us, is like a firebrand dropped into the sea, where it would certainly be quenched were it not of such a miraculous quality that it baffles the waters and sets up its reign of fire and light even in the depths.

Salvation by grace, through faith, is not of ourselves in the sense of being the result of our own power. We are bound to view salvation as being a divine act as surely as we do creation or providence or resurrection. In every point of the process of salvation, these words aree appropriate: *"not of yourselves."* From the first desire for it to the full reception of it by faith, it is forever of the Lord alone, and not of ourselves. The man believes, but that belief is only one result among many of the implantation of divine life within the man's soul by God Himself.

> **There is no continuity between the states of nature and of grace; one is darkness, the other light.**

Even the very will or desire to be saved by grace is *"not of yourselves: it is the gift of God."* Here lies the emphasis of the discussion. A man ought to believe in Jesus. It is his duty to receive Him whom God has set forth to be a propitiation for sins. Yet, man will not believe in Jesus. He prefers anything to faith in his Redeemer. Unless the Spirit of God convinces his judgment and constrains his will, man has no heart to believe in Jesus unto eternal life.

I ask any saved man to look back upon his own conversion and explain how it came about. You turned to

Christ and believed on His name; these were your own acts and deeds. But, what caused you to turn that way? What sacred force was it that turned you from sin to righteousness? Do you attribute this singular renewal to the existence of a something better in you than has been yet discovered in your unconverted neighbor? No, you confess that you might have been what he is now if it had not been that there was a potent something that touched the spring of your will, enlightened your understanding, and guided you to the foot of the cross. Gratefully we confess the fact; it must be so. Salvation by grace, through faith, is not of ourselves. None of us would dream of taking any honor to ourselves from our conversion or from any gracious effect that has flowed from the first divine cause.

It Is the Gift of God

Finally, salvation may be called, *Theodora*, or God's gift, and each saved soul may be surnamed *Dorothea,* which is another form of the same expression. Multiply your phrases and expand your expositions as you will, but salvation truly traced to its fountainhead is all contained in the unspeakable gift—the free, unmeasured blessing of love.

Salvation is the gift of God, in opposition to wages. When a man pays another his wages, he does what is right. No one would dream of praising him for it. Yet, we praise God for salvation because it is

Grace

not the payment of debt but the gift of grace. No man enters eternal life on earth or in heaven as his due: *"It is the gift of God."* We say, "Nothing is freer than a gift." Salvation is so purely, so absolutely a gift of God that nothing can be freer.

God gives salvation because He chooses to give it, according to that grand text that has made many a man bite his lip in wrath: *"I will have mercy on whom I will have mercy, and I will have compassion on whom I will have compassion"* (Romans 9:15). You are all guilty and condemned, and the Great King pardons whom He chooses from among you. This is His royal prerogative. He saves in infinite sovereignty of grace.

At the same time, the Lord Himself has declared, *"Whosoever shall call upon the name of the Lord shall be saved"* (Acts 2:21). This sweeping statement in no way conflicts with the statement that no one receives salvation except as a gift. You must stand obliged to God's mercy for it, or else you will die without it. To pretend a right to it would be to insult God, whose heart is set upon the exercise of His free bounty. He will not barter and bargain with you—so much grace for so many tears, so much mercy for so much repentance, so much love for so many works—the idea is contemptible. Salvation is not on the market except under these explicit terms: *"without money and without price"* (Isaiah 55:1). Freely may you be saved if you will cast out of your soul the last thought of making God your debtor.

All of Grace

Salvation is the gift of God—that is to say, it is completely so, in opposition to the notion of growth. Salvation is not a natural production from within; it is brought from a foreign zone and planted within the heart by heavenly hands. Salvation is a gift from God in its entirety. If you will receive it, there it is, complete.

Will you accept it as a perfect gift? "No, I will produce it in my own workshop." You cannot forge a work so rare and costly, upon which even Jesus spent His life's blood. Here is a garment without seam, woven from the top down in one piece. It will cover you and make you glorious. Will you take it and wear it? "No, I will sit at the loom, and I will weave a raiment of my own!" Proud fool that you are! You spin cobwebs. You weave a dream. Oh, that you would freely take what Christ upon the cross declared to be finished.

> **God will not barter with you; salvation is on the market only under His terms.**

"It is the gift of God" in the sense that it is eternally secure, in opposition to the gifts of men, which soon pass away. *"Not as the world giveth, give I unto you"* (John 14:27), said our Lord Jesus. If my Lord Jesus gives you salvation at this moment, you have it, and you have it forever. He will never take it back again. And if He does not take it from you, who can? If He saves you now through faith, you are saved—so

saved that you will never perish, neither will anyone pluck you out of His hand (John 10:28).

I pray that you may know, at this moment and always, the joy of being eternally secure as you *"abide under the shadow of the Almighty"* (Psalm 91:1) because you have accepted His free, merciful gift of salvation by His precious grace.

Chapter Five

Grace for the Covenanter

Five

Grace for
the Covenanter

*All the paths of the LORD are mercy and truth unto such as keep
his covenant and his testimonies.*
—Psalm 25:10

This Psalm is intensely earnest. *"Unto thee, O
LORD, do I lift up my soul"* (v. 1). The sentences
are ingots of gold. Every word is exceedingly
weighty with feeling and sincerity. One reason for this
weightiness is the fact that David was suffering affliction. He said, *"I am desolate and afflicted....Look upon mine
affliction and my pain"* (vv. 16, 18).

Pain can be a great disenchanter. Flowery speeches
suit the summer of our health, but we do not find them
in the winter of our grief. Pain kills fine phrases as a
mighty frost kills butterflies and moths. You can play
with religion until you are laid low, and then it becomes

serious work. The romance of religion is one thing; the reality of it is another. It would be a great blessing to some if they were shriveled with a little pain, or else they will grow unbearable in their pride. Often the best thing that can happen to us is that we are reduced to our true selves and not left to strut about as noble somebodies. May our meditations be solid and leave no tinge of unreality in our minds!

Also mixed with David's suffering, there was a sense of sin. Read the eleventh verse of that same Psalm: *"For thy name's sake, O LORD, pardon mine iniquity; for it is great."* A little further we find: *"Forgive all my sins"* (v. 18). No man can have a worse troubling of soul than when under conviction of sin. A thorn in the flesh is nothing in comparison to a thorn in the conscience.

> **The romance of religion is one thing; the reality of it is another.**

A sense of sin is another great disenchanter. This bursts the bubbles of conceit by the thousands. When the heart is awakened and sin is laid bare by the Spirit of God so that we are truly humbled by it, life ceases to be sport, and an awful earnestness pervades the core of our being. To carry burning coals in the bosom is nothing compared to bearing sin in an awakened conscience. There is no cheating the soul when sin lies hard on it, and no attempt is then made at dealing with God in a dishonest or superficial manner. Crushed into the dust, we pine for a real atonement, a real faith, and the true seal of the Spirit to make our pardon sure. When sin is truly felt, we come before the great Father, not with mimicking sorrow, but with downright, soul-felt weeping and breaking hearts. Thus, we cry to Him, *"God be merciful to me a sinner"* (Luke 18:13).

If we feel either of these two things, pain or sin—and who among us can hope to be without them at all times?—then we will see the solemn side of life and look for those sure consolations by which we may be sustained. I hope that this subject of discussion may help in that direction.

One other thing is notable about David in writing the Psalm in which our text is found: Whatever his trouble might have been and however deep his sense of sin was, he always looked to God. He cried, *"Unto thee, O LORD, do I lift up my soul"* (Psalm 25:1), and, *"Remember thou me for thy goodness' sake, O LORD"* (v. 7). In our text verse, his mind focused on *"the paths of the LORD."*

> **A thorn in the flesh is nothing in comparison to a thorn in the conscience.**

The ungodly fly away from God when He chastens them, but saints kiss the chastening rod. The child of God goes home when it grows dark. We seek our healing from the hand that has wounded us.

Which way do you look in a storm? If the Lord is now your haven, you will look to Him in the last dread storm, for that is the way your eye has turned all these years. If you look to God for everything, you are looking out of the right window. When your eyes look toward the great sea of divine all-sufficiency, you do not look in vain. You may have to come again seven more times before you see your deliverance; and when you do see it, it may seem no bigger than a man's hand. (See 1 Kings 18:41–45.) However, you will not be ashamed in the end.

I trust that this mark and evidence of being a child of God is upon you. If it is so, you are among the Lord's army, whom I would call to the battle. With your face set straight ahead and your eyes focused on our Captain, come with me to the rallying place of the Lord of Hosts.

In our text verse, I see two things worth addressing. The first is the character of people who are in covenant with God: *"such as keep his covenant and his testimonies."* The second is the notable experience of such individuals: *"All the paths of the LORD are mercy and truth unto such as keep his covenant."*

The Spiritual Covenanter

Observe in the text the footprint of the spiritual covenanter. We may define spiritual covenanters as people who enter into covenant with God, who are the recipients of His grace, who are the beneficiaries of the Lord's last will and testament, and who are *"such as keep his covenant and his testimonies."*

Grace

You may have heard of the old Covenanters of Scotland, their decisiveness of mind and force of character. Their theory of government for the kingdom of Scotland was quaintly impractical, but it grew out of a true and deep fear of the Lord. The Old Testament combative spirit in them was not balanced enough with the meekness of Christ, or else they would not have touched the weapon of steel. Yet, in this mistake they were very far from being alone.

In my bedroom, I have hung up a painting of an old Covenanter. He sits in a wild glen with his Bible open before him on a huge stone. He leans on his great broad sword, and his horse stands quietly at his side. Evidently, he senses the battle afar off and is preparing for it by drinking in some mighty promise. As I look into the old man's face, I can almost hear him saying to himself, "For the crown of Christ and the covenant, I would gladly lay down my life this day."

The ungodly flee when God chastens them, but saints kiss the chastening rod.

The Covenanters did lay down their lives, too, very gloriously, and Scotland owes to her covenanting fathers far more than she knows. It was a grand day in which they spread the *Solemn League and Covenant* on the tombstones of the old churchyard in Edinburgh, and all sorts of men came forward to set their names to it. Glorious was that roll of worthy men. There were the lords of the Covenant and the common men of the Covenant. Some pricked a vein and dipped the pen into their blood that they might write their names with the very fluid of their hearts.

All over England, there were also men who entered into a similar solemn league and covenant; they met together to worship God according to the light they were given and not according to human order-of-service books. They were united in resolution about this one thing: that Rome should not come back to power while they could lift a hand against her, and neither should any

> **The true covenanter has resolved to be on living terms with the true God for time and eternity.**

other power in throne or Parliament prevent the free exercise of their consciences for Christ's cause and covenant.

These stern old men with their stiff notions have gone, but what do we have in their places? Indifference and frivolity. We have no Roundheads and Puritans, but we arrange flowers and play lawn tennis! We have no contentions for the faith because our amusements occupy all our time. This wonderful century has become a child and put away manly things. Self-disciplined men, men of integrity and true grit, are now very few and far between as compared with the old covenanting days.

Grace

In Right Relationship with God

However, I do not want to discuss the old Covenanters but rather those who at this time keep the covenant of the Lord. I pray to God that we have among us great companies of believers, *"such as keep his covenant, and...remember his commandments to do them"* (Psalm 103:18).

The true covenanter is one who has found God and, in that, has made the greatest discovery that was ever made. He has discovered not only a god, but the living and true God, and has resolved to be on living terms with Him for time and for eternity. Henceforth, he will never shut his eyes to God, for his longing is to see more and more of Him. He is determined to be right with God; he knows that if he were right with all his fellow creatures and everything about him and yet were wrong with God, he would be out of order in the main point. He has settled in his own soul that he will know the Lord, be right with Him, at peace with Him, and in league with Him.

It is not natural for men thus to cling to God and seek after Him, but it has become natural for this man so that he hungers and thirsts for the living God. By this very fact the man is ennobled. He is lifted up above the brutes that perish. A man capable of the idea of covenant with God, and caught up with a passion for it, must surely be born from above. There must be a divine nature within him, or he would not be drawn toward the Divine One above him. It is true: The Spirit of God has been working in his heart.

Grace for the Covenanter

Experience with the First Covenant

Already, too, the man has discovered a prior covenant, whose ruins lay between him and God and had blocked the road. Turning to his Bible, the believer finds that we had been under the first covenant in our relationship with God. He reads of the first covenant, the covenant with our first father, Adam, which was broken by his disobedience, whose fatal breach has brought upon us losses and woes innumerable.

The true believer has not ignored this first covenant or made short confession of it, for he himself has felt his share in its failure and has come under its condemnation. His very desire to be right with God has brought home to him the judgment of the law; he has smarted under the lash of it. He has seen the Lord arrayed in robes of justice, avenging the breaches of His covenant, and he has thought to himself, "What shall I do? The law is holy, and the commandment holy and just and good; but I am carnal, sold under sin."

Beloved, we are condemned under the first covenant, not only by the act of our representative, Adam, but also through our personal endorsement of his rebellion by our own actual sin. That covenant, which should have been a covenant of life, has become a covenant of death to us.

You know what I mean. I am addressing many who know by deep personal experience what it is to be the prisoners of the covenant, shut up in soul despair and numbered for destruction. The future was against you; you knew you could not keep the law, even though you wished and prayed you could. The past was against you; as for former violations of the law, you could find no way to make amends for them. The present was against you; your inward corruptions were continually gnawing at your heart like the worm that never dies (Isaiah 66:24) and the leach that is never satisfied (Proverbs 30:15). Yet, despite all this, you still followed after the Lord and could not live without Him.

Perception of a Better Covenant

The covenanter I am describing is one who has, through divine enlightenment, perceived a better covenant and the sure salvation contained therein. He has seen in the Lord Jesus a Second Adam, greater than the first, and he has heard the glorious Lord exclaim, *"I the LORD...give* [Him] *for a covenant of the people"* (Isaiah 42:6). He has seen Jesus pledge unto God to make good the breaches of the broken covenant. The believer has seen the Son of God arrayed in bloodstained garments coming from Gethsemane and has seen Him answering at the bar for the broken law, scourged with *"the chastisement of our peace"* (Isaiah 53:5) and bound with the chains of our condemnation. The covenanter has seen the beloved Surety of the new covenant meeting the law's demands at Calvary, surrendering His hands to be nailed for our ill-doings, His feet to be

> **Holiness is the passion of a true believer.**

fastened up for our wanderings, and His heart to be pierced for our wantonness.

O my dear souls, have you seen our Lord stripped for sin amid the tempest of divine wrath? Have you heard Him cry, *"My God, my God, why hast thou forsaken me"* (Matthew 27:46)? If so, you have seen how out of the old covenant the new was born, like life from between the jaws of death. Our souls have stood in the midst of the horrible tempest, half-blinded by the lightning and deafened by the thunder. At last there has been a rent in the black mantle; a shower of wondrous love has followed the black tempest; and a voice has been heard, sweeter than the harps of angels, crying, *"It is finished"* (John 19:30).

Thus have the Lord's covenanted ones come forth from under the old covenant into the new covenant of grace in which peace and joy abound. Now are we in happy league with God. Now we can think, feel, and act in harmony with God. Our covenant with Him will encompass all our lives. We are His, and He is ours: *"The LORD is my portion, saith my soul"* (Lamentations 3:24). Yet, on the other hand, *"The LORD's portion is his people"* (Deuteronomy 32:9). Henceforth, we have no life apart from the living God; He is our ambition and our expectation, our end and our way, our desire and our delight. He rejoices over us (see Zephaniah 3:17) to do us good, and we rejoice in Him and seek His glory.

Grace

A Heart Covenant with God

The spiritual covenanter has the covenant with God written on the tablet of his heart. I have known believers who, when first converted, have followed a hint given them by Dr. Doddridge in his *Rise and Progress of Religion,* where he drew up a covenant that he invited the reader to sign. Some have executed a deed with great solemnity and have also observed the day of its signature from year to year. Very proper, no doubt, for some natures, but I fear that to the more timid and conscientious such covenants are apt to cause bondage. When they find that they have not, in all things, lived up to their own pledges, they are apt to cut themselves off from all part and lot in the matter. This is the covenant of works and not of grace, a covenant on paper and not the covenant written upon the heart and mind.

The true covenanter wills the will of God. It is not merely that God commands him to do right, but he longs to do it. God's law is his love. (See Psalm 119:97.) That which is pleasing to God is pleasing to His people, because their hearts are made like His own. The divine likeness is restored by the Spirit of grace; hence, the will of the Lord is written upon the newly born nature. Holiness is the passion of a true believer. He consents and assents to the law that it is good, and the divine life within him delights itself *"in the law of the Lord"* (Psalm 1:2).

Grace for the Covenanter

The surest sort of covenant is this divine writing in the new nature, according to these gracious promises:

A new heart also will I give you, and a new spirit will I put within you: and I will take away the stony heart out of your flesh, and I will give you an heart of flesh.
(Ezekiel 36:26)

But this shall be the covenant that I will make with the house of Israel; after those days, saith the LORD, I will put my law in their inward parts, and write it in their hearts; and will be their God, and they shall be my people. (Jeremiah 31:33)

Happy is the man whose covenant with God is the covenant of his own desire, who wills and wishes and longs and labors to yield himself fully and wholly to the law of his God!

United with the Lord

This covenanting man does not regard himself any more as one by himself, because he *"is joined unto the Lord"* (1 Corinthians 6:17) and has entered into the closest fellowship with Him. None can separate him from God; the union is vital and complete. He has thrown his little all into God's great all, and he has taken God's great all unto himself to be his heritage forever. Now, henceforth, he is in God and God in him. (See John 14:20.)

You ask me what it is that thus binds a man to God. My answer is that he feels he is henceforth joined unto the Lord for many reasons, among them being that the Lord has chosen him to be His own. He is old-fashioned enough to believe that God has a choice in the salvation of men, and he perceives that the Lord has evidently chosen him for salvation, for faith has been granted to him. He often cries, "Why me? Why me?" Yet he knows that those whom the Lord calls by grace He first predestined to that end (Romans 8:30), and he is not ashamed to believe in his election. The

> **He who is chosen of God chooses God and does so because he has been chosen.**

man who believes that God has chosen him is the man who enters into covenant with God and keeps that covenant. He who is chosen of God chooses God; he chooses God because he has been chosen. The vows of God are upon him. Such amazing grace compels him to a consecrated life.

The Mark of Redemption

Moreover, in addition to the choice of God, this covenanter sees the mark of Christ's blood upon his body, soul, and spirit. The redemption made on the cross, whatever its other directions, is seen by the believer to be especially for him. He cries, "For me was the bloody sweat; for me the spitting and the scourging; for me the nails and the spear. Truly I am not my own, for I am bought with a price."

This blood-bought man feels that he cannot be as other men are. He must pledge with his hand unto the

God of Jacob, and he must cling to and confess that he belongs to the Lord alone.

Others may be their own lords. But, as for us, we have been redeemed, not *"with corruptible things, as silver and gold,...but with the precious blood of Christ"* (1 Peter 1:18–19). O beloved, if you know your election and your redemption, you must and will dedicate yourselves unto the Lord by a covenant that cannot be broken. If the choice of the Father and the redemption of the Son do not supply us with a potent force toward holiness, what can do so? Well may we be the covenanted ones of God when we are thus distinguished.

The Subject of a Special Calling

In addition, the covenanting believer feels that he has been the subject of a special call. Whatever God may have done with others, he knows that God has dealt specially with him according to His grace and mercy. The Lord has said to him,

> *Fear not: for I have redeemed thee, I have called thee by thy name; thou art mine....Since thou wast precious in my sight, thou hast been honourable, and I have loved thee.*   (Isaiah 43:1, 4)

A voice has called him from his kindred and from his father's house, just as surely as Abraham was called. The Lord Himself has brought him *"out of darkness into his marvellous light"* (1 Peter 2:9). Whatever the Gospel may be to the congregation at large, it has been *"the power of God unto salvation"* (Romans 1:16) for him. In it he has felt the touch of a hand unfelt before and heard the sound of a voice unheard in all the days gone by. Omnipotent grace has aroused the echoes of his soul: *"When thou saidest, Seek ye my face; my heart said unto thee, Thy face, LORD, will I seek"* (Psalm 27:8).

This special, authoritative calling is another mighty reason for entering into league and covenant with God. Let your prayer be: "By that omnipotent call, O Lord, I render up myself to You. Let the world do as it wants—I cannot account for its folly—*'but as for me and my house, we will serve the LORD'* (Joshua 24:15)." Our bonds of friendship with the world are broken, whatever it may do or say. We are bound to the Lord forever by the same power that has pulled us out of our former slavery. With election, redemption, and calling, what more can I say?

United to God in Christ Jesus

Yes, I can add something more, for the true covenanter feels that he is now united to God in Christ Jesus. What a matchless doctrine is unity with God through Jesus Christ! No man knows the lineage and the nature of the man who has been quickened by the Spirit. You cannot tell his ancestry or his progeny. We talk of aristocrats, but believers are the aristocrats of heaven and earth. We often hear the words "royalty" and "blood royal." The true blood royal of the universe is in the man who believes in Jesus. He has *"made us unto our God kings and priests"* (Revelation 5:10). By virtue of our union with Christ, we are one with God and *partakers of the divine nature*" (2 Peter 1:4).

The day will come when all the baubles and trappings of courts will be laid aside as the faded tawdriness they are. When that happens, the real dignity and honor of the twice-born, the quickened by the Holy Spirit, will truly be seen. To be members of the body of Christ means glory indeed. To be married to the King's Son, to the Lord Jesus, means such a state of bliss that even angels cannot reach it. Given such an immeasurable privilege, do you question that a man enters into a sure covenant with God?

Zeal for the Gospel

There are several more things I would like to say briefly about this true covenanter. May the Lord make each one of us to be of his character! You may know him by his attachment to the Lord Jesus, who is the Sum, Substance, Surety, and Seal of the covenant. The committed believer is known also by his zeal for the Gospel, through which the covenant is revealed to the sons of men. He will not hear anything that is not according to the old Gospel, for he counts any other gospel to be a deadly evil. He is very fond of the word *grace,* and with grace itself he is altogether enamored.

The person who is in covenant with God cannot bear the idea of human merit—he loathes it. It raises his indignation. I have known some Christians who come out from hearing certain apathetic sermons with their souls on fire with holy wrath. I feel, in casting my eye over many modern writings, as if I were about to die from breathing poisonous gas. We cannot endure the smell of false piety and human righteousness. Others may feed on philosophical morality, but nothing but the grace of God will do for us. Stray dogs may feed on any rubbish, but men of God must live on the grace of God and nothing else. Our keeping the covenant and the testimonies binds us to a firm adherence to the inspired Gospel and to the grace of God, which is the glory of it.

> **Believers are the aristocrats of heaven and earth.**

A Person of Faith

He who is indeed in covenant with God is known by his continual regard for the life, walk, and triumph of faith. He has faith, and by that faith he lives and grows. He is, has, and does all things by faith. No one can tempt him away from the faith in which he stands. Carnal sense and fleshly feeling are not able to tempt him from believing. The highest enjoyment proffered by a fancied perfection cannot charm him from standing by faith. "No," he says, "I must trust, or else it is all over with me. My element is faith. Just as a fish out of water dies, so do I die—and all my covenanting with God dies, too—unless I cling by faith to the promise of a faithful God." Even if all other men should live by their senses and emotions, the true covenanter will not quit the hallowed way of faith in the Lord.

Grace for the Covenanter

Proclaiming the Pure Gospel

This covenanting man will also be known by his stern resolve to preserve the Gospel in its purity and hand it on to others. When the truth of God was made known to Abraham, it was committed to him and to his descendants as a sacred deposit, of which they were to be the guardians and trustees. It was theirs to keep that lamp burning, by which the rest of the world would, in due time, be saved from darkness. The eternal truths of the Gospel of our Lord Jesus Christ are given over to certain chosen men and women to be preserved by them until the coming of the Lord. This keeping is to be accompanied with a constant proclamation, so that the truth may spread as well as live, and may continue to conquer.

You who are the covenanted ones of God, do not let His Gospel suffer damage. I charge you who love the Lord to bind the Gospel about you more firmly than ever. Bear aloft the standard of our grand army. The bloodstained colors of the cross—carry them to the front, spread them on every wind, uplift them on every hill! And if you cannot spread the truth but are instead locked up for defending it, then do so even to the death. Wrap the colors about your heart. If you cannot live to bear them as your flag, be wrapped in them as your shroud!

A true covenanter says, "Sooner death than to be false of faith." The crown of our Lord Jesus will never suffer loss. We will do everything for Jesus. We will for

His sake bear reproach (Hebrews 13:13), and for His sake we will labor to win souls unto God. We vow that He will be glorified in our mortal bodies (1 Corinthians 6:20). We further state that, by some means, His great name will be made known to the ends of the earth (Psalm 48:10).

O my fellow warriors! I am invigorated by the very thought of you. God still has His faithful covenanters who have not bowed the knee to Baal, to whom the Lord is God and King forever and ever.

The Experience of the Covenanter

For our second part of this study, let us now consider the covenanter's extraordinary experience. Our text verse says, *"All the paths of the LORD are mercy and truth unto such as keep his covenant and his testimonies."* Those who keep the covenant walk in blessing.

The Lord Approaches in Many Ways

Observe, first, that the Lord makes many approaches to covenanting men. He does not leave them alone, but He comes to them and manifests Himself to them. By the expression, *"All the paths of the LORD,"* I learn that the Lord has many ways of drawing near to His chosen. Not only in the public highways of grace does He meet those with whom He is on terms of peace, but in many private and secret paths. In a grassy field a path is made by constant treading, and God makes paths to His people by continually drawing near to their souls and communing with them. The Lord has many paths, for He comes to them from different points of the compass as their experience requires. He sometimes uses this way and sometimes another, in order that He may commune with us. He will never leave His covenanted ones alone for long. He often says, *"Gather my saints together unto me; those that have made a covenant with me by sacrifice"* (Psalm 50:5).

I like the word *paths* as it is translated in our text verse, for it seems to say that the Lord has walks of His own. He makes ways for Himself and goes along them quietly, taking His people unaware. All of a sudden, He whispers a word of heavenly promise, and then He is gone again. However, He is not gone for long. He makes another path and comes to us with new anointing and fresh revelation. His visits to us are many and gracious.

> **God does not leave His children alone but manifests Himself to them.**

O beloved, if you will give yourself to God, God will give Himself to you. Youthful one, I invite you to the grand destiny of one who will henceforth live with God, to whom God will manifest Himself. Would not this be a distinguished honor? Do not think it unattainable. God may be reached; if you will consecrate yourself to Him this day by a covenant through Jesus

Grace

Christ, the ever-blessed Sacrifice, you will know the visitations of the Almighty. You will, like Enoch, walk with God (Genesis 5:24).

Believe me, this is the solemn truth. Between this place and the pearly gates, the Lord will come to you and will take up His abode with you. When you cannot get to Him, He will come to you, for He is a great path-maker. His ways are in the sea, and He leaps over the mountains. He has a desire for the work of His hands, and that desire will break through stone walls to reach you. How blessed is the one to whom the Lord makes innumerable paths! What happiness floods that soul!

Merciful Treatment

Note, next, that all the dealings of God with His people are in mercy: *"All the paths of the LORD are mercy."* This is fitting, for the best of the saints will always need mercy. Those who keep His covenant are still kept by His mercy. When they grow in grace and come to be fully developed Christians, they still need mercy for their sins, their weaknesses, and their needs. The Lord exercises mercy to the most highly instructed believer as well as to the babe in grace, mercy to the most useful worker as much as to the most weary sufferer. *"O give thanks unto the LORD, for he is good: for his mercy endureth for ever"* (Psalm 107:1).

That mercy will always be *"tender mercy"* (Luke 1:78), abiding mercy, and *"abundant mercy"* (1 Peter 1:3). His mercy is as constant as the day, as fresh as the hour, and *"new every morning"* (Lamentations 3:23). Mercy covers all His works (Psalm 145:9). In every gift of providence and in every way of predestination, mercy may be seen. It would be greatly advantageous for us to meditate more on the mercy of God to us. So much of His mercy comes and goes without our noticing it. It is a shame that the Lord should thus be deprived of the revenues of His praise!

The original Hebrew word that has been translated *paths* means "well-worn roads" or "wheel tracks," such ruts as wagons make when they go down our green roads in wet weather and sink in up to the axles. God's ways are at times like heavy wagon tracks that cut deep into our souls, yet all of them are merciful. Whether our days trip along like the angels mounting on Jacob's ladder to heaven or grind along like the wagons that Joseph sent for Jacob, they are in each case ordered by God's mercy.

When I recall the happy memories of a tried past, as I walk down a summery green lane and look at the deep ruts that God's providence made long ago, I see flowers of mercies growing in them. All of the crushing and crashing was in goodness. *"Surely goodness and mercy* [have] *follow*[ed] *me all the days of my life"* (Psalm 23:6)—yes, in *"all the days of my life,"* the dark and cloudy, the stormy and the wintry, as surely as in *"the days of heaven upon the earth"* (Deuteronomy 11:21). Beloved, we may sing a song of untainted mercy. The paths of God have been to us nothing else but mercy. Mercy, mercy,

mercy! *"I will sing of the mercies of the LORD for ever"* (Psalm 89:1).

Grace in His Truth

The psalmist said, *"All the paths of the LORD are mercy and truth."* That is to say, God has always shown the truth of His Word. He has never been false to His pledge. He has done according to His Word. Moreover, the blessings that God has promised have always turned out to be as He represented them. We have followed no cunningly devised fables. The blessings of grace are not fancies or frenzies, exaggerations or mere sentiments. The Lord has never fallen short of His promise. He has never kept His word to the ear and broken it to the heart.

> **The paths of God have been nothing else to us but mercy.**

All the ways of God have not only been merciful and true, but they have been essential *"mercy and truth."* We have had truth-filled mercy; authentic mercy; substantial, solid, essential mercy.

I have found no delusion in trusting in God. I may have been a dreamer in some things, but when I have lived for God, I have then exercised the shrewdest common sense and have walked after the rule of prudence. It is no vain thing to serve God; the vanity lies on the other side.

Grace for the Covenanter

Many think the Christian experience leans toward the area of sentiment, if not of imagination, but indeed it is not so. The surest fact in a believer's life is God's nearness to him, care for him, and love for him. Other things are shadows or impressions that come and go, but the goodness of God is the substance, the truth, the reality of life. How much I desire to persuade you of this! But, alas, the natural mind cannot receive spiritual things (1 Corinthians 2:14). I may bear witness of that which I taste and handle, but you will not believe me. Divine Spirit, come and open blind eyes.

No Exceptions

There is no exception to this rule: *"All the paths of the LORD are mercy and truth unto such as keep his covenant."* They say there is no rule without an exception, but there is an exception to that rule. All God's dealings with His people are gracious and faithful. Sometimes the ways of God are full of truth and mercy manifestly; they have been so to me in many notable instances.

I hope I do not trouble you too often with personal experiences. I do not write of them out of egotism, but I do so because it seems to me that every Christian should add his own personal testimony to the great evidence that proves the truth of our God. If I tell you about John Newton, you may answer, "He is dead, and you did not know him." However, if I tell you of Charles Haddon Spurgeon, I know him and can give his account truthfully.

Grace

About ten days ago, I was called to bear a baptism of pain. I had a night of anguish, and the pangs did not cease in the morning. How gladly I would have escaped from these acute attacks, but it seemed I might not hope it. I felt worn down and spent. Late in the morning, my ever-thoughtful secretary came by my bedside and cheered me greatly by the news that the mail brought tidings of considerable help for the various ministries. In fact, there was far more coming in than is at all usual at this season. A generous legacy was reported that was to be shared between the orphanage and the college. Another will named the orphanage as a secondary legatee. Living friends had also sent large sums in what seemed to be a directed concert of liberality. They had no way of knowing that their friend was going to be very ill that morning, but the Lord knew, and He moved them to take away every care from me. It seemed to me as if my Lord said, "Now, you are not going to fret and worry while you are ill. You will have no temptation to do so, for I will send you in so much help for all My work that you will not dare to be downcast." Truly in this, the paths of the Lord were mercy and truth to me.

Many times have I been lost in wonder at the Lord's mercy to His unworthy servant. I bow my head and bless the name of the Lord and cry, "Why is this to me?" Beloved, one can bear rheumatism or gout when mercy flows in as a flood. *"Shall we receive good at the hand of God, and shall we not receive evil?"* (Job 2:10). Seeing that it all comes from the same hand, we should receive it with equal cheerfulness. I am thus enabled to suffer with patience and endure with tranquillity, *"because God hath dealt graciously with me"* (Genesis 33:11).

I have often found that His comfort abounds to me in proportion to my tribulations. Of course, I am on the lookout for the mercy when I begin to feel the pain, even as a child looks for the sweet when he finds himself called upon to take medicine. Those more closely around me say, "Now that you have a bad time of personal suffering, you will see the Lord doing wonderfully for you." They are not disappointed.

Indeed, I serve a good Master. I can speak well of Him at all times, but I find Him especially kind when the weather is rough around His pilgrim child! Have you not found it so in your life? Come, dear friends, you may not be able to tell me what the Lord has done personally in your lives, but I exhort you to speak when you have had your dinners and your children are gathered around you. Tell them how gracious God has been to you in your times of trouble. I urge you to recall your memories of His great goodness often.

> **One can bear any illness when mercy flows in as a flood.**

Unseen Mercies

Be aware that even when we cannot see it, the Lord is just as merciful in His ways to us. We may not expect to be indulged and pampered by always being allowed to see the mercy of God, like silly children who pout unless their father stuffs their mouths with sweets and their hands with toys. God is as good when He denies as when He grants. Though we often see the marvelous tenderness of our God, it is not necessary that we see it to make it true. Our God is wise as a father and tender as a mother. While we cannot comprehend His methods, we still believe in His love. This is not false trust but a solid confidence to which the Lord is fully entitled. There can be no doubt that *"all the paths of the* LORD *are mercy and truth unto such as keep his covenant."*

I hear some say, "These things do not happen to me. I find myself struggling alone and full of sorrow." Do you keep the covenant? Some of you professing Christian people live however you please and not by covenant rule. You do not live for God, you do not keep His covenant, you do not observe His testimonies, and you are not living consecrated lives. Therefore, if you do not enjoy His mercy and His truth, do not blame the Lord. The verse says that all His paths are mercy and truth *"unto such as keep his covenant."* Remember the character, and do not expect the blessing apart from it. O child of God, be more careful to keep the way of the Lord, more concentrated in heart in seeking His glory, and you will see the loving-kindness and the tender mercy of the Lord in your life. God bless this feeble testimony of mine to all who learn of it!

Grace for the Covenanter

The Joy of Being in Covenant with God

I have this much to add to it: What a bliss it is to have entered upon the spiritual life and to be in covenant with God! Even if there were no mercy of a providential character joined to the covenant, it would nevertheless be the grandest thing that could ever happen to any one of us to be living for God. What solidity we have in godliness! It puts eternal rock beneath our feet.

There are fascinating things in life about which you are almost afraid to inquire, for fear they should not prove to be what they seem. All earthborn joys are of this kind: Their charms are on the surface; their beauty is skin deep. But, regarding the life consecrated to God by covenant and then enriched by His mercy, you may pry and dig and search, and the more you do so, the more will you be certain that now you are in the land of realities.

God's comfort abounds to us in proportion to our tribulations.

Though we do not see physically, we perceive with a perception clearer than sight, and so we will perceive through life. When they fling back those golden gates and we peer into the spiritual realm, then we will value most of all the life that observes the covenant and is surrounded with mercy and truth. What a wondrous thing the life of a consecrated man will seem to be when we will view it in its completeness, in the light of the eternal throne! Then will the embroidery of love be seen in its beauty, and the fabric of life will be admitted to be worthy of God. Things not seen as yet will be seen then, and things known in part will be seen in all their fullness (1 Corinthians 13:12). I suppose that one of the engagements of heaven will be to observe how kindly our God has dealt with us upon the road. At any rate, when we come to the glory land, only the life that was spent in communion with God will we deem to have been true life. Link us with God, and we live; divide us from Him, and we are dead.

A Vision of Life Without Grace

I hear worldlings mutter, "Where is this man coming from? We know nothing and care nothing about being in covenant with God." You who live for gain or pleasure, truly you despise the life I set before you, but it is your own way of life that most deserves scorn! I will sketch for you with the pencil of truth. It is a country scene that passed by my mind's eye but a few hours ago. I sat by the water's edge, at a point where abundant springs poured forth new streams. It was a brook, wide but shallow, and the pure water glided along refreshingly under the overhanging boughs. Little children were there, wading into the stream and enjoying its cool waters.

One of them was a true representative of many wealthy merchants. He went fishing with a bright green glass bottle, and his ventures were successful. Again and again, I heard his voice ring out most joyously and impressively, "Look here! Look here! Such a big 'un! I have caught such a big 'un!" It was by no means a whale that he held up, but a fish that might have been an inch long at most. How he triumphed: "Such a big 'un!" To him the affairs of nations were nothing when compared with the great spoil that he had taken.

This lad symbolizes the gentleman who has made a successful speculation in the stock exchange. For the next few days, he astonishes everybody as they hear that it was "Such a big one!" Earth and heaven and hell, time and eternity, may all admire the accomplishment now that the glass bottle contains its prey.

> **Even when we cannot see it, the Lord is just as merciful in His ways to us.**

His brother, not far off, changed the picture for me. He was less richly endowed, and yet he had a very serviceable tin can with which he fished most diligently. Soon I heard his voice, pitched in another key: "Nasty little things! They won't come here! I can't catch 'em! They're good for nothing! I won't try any more." Then the impetuous genius threw his tin can with a splash into the water, and his enterprise was ended.

This boy represents the merchant whose business has closed or whose goods will not command a market. Things will not come his way. He cannot get ahead. He has failed miserably, and it has been published in the gazette. He is convinced that all society is out of order, or he would have been sure to succeed. He is sick of it all for the present.

You smile at my boys! O worldlings, they are yourselves! You are those children, and your ambitions are their little amusements.

O happy man that lives on high,
While men lie groveling here.

Without God you are paddling in the stream of life, fishing for minnows. If you get a hold on God, because He has laid hold on you, blessed one, there is then a soul in you. Then you have come to be allied with angels and akin to seraphim. Apart from God, you subside into shameful littleness.

O Lord Jesus, have compassion on those who do not know You! Amen.

Chapter Six

Twelve Covenant Mercies

Six
Twelve
Covenant Mercies

Incline your ear, and come unto me: hear, and your soul shall live;
and I will make an everlasting covenant with you, even
the sure mercies of David.
—Isaiah 55:3

So far, I have pleaded with all to come to God, to hear what He has to say, to give diligent and earnest heed to His teaching about their souls and about salvation. As I have pleaded—and I can truly say, with all the strength I have—I have made this one of the master arguments: that, in hearing, their souls would live, and in coming to God, they would find Him ready to enter into *"an everlasting covenant...even the sure mercies of David"* with them.

That seems to me to be one of the most astonishing truths that was ever given to men to realize:

that God would be a high contracting party with poor, insignificant, guilty man; that He would make a covenant with man, with you and me; and that He would bind Himself by a solemn promise, give His sacred pledge, and enter into a holy contract of mercy with the guilty sons of Adam. I believe that, if men were in their right minds and God had taught their reason to be reasonable, they would be drawn to the Lord by such a wonderful promise as this: *"I will make an everlasting covenant with you, even the sure mercies of David."*

Remember, there was a covenant of old that men broke. The covenant of works was essentially as follows: Do this, and you will live; keep this and that commandment, and you will be rewarded. That covenant failed because man did not keep God's commands, and so he did not earn the promised reward. We broke the terms of that contract, and it is no longer valid, except that we come under penalty for the breach of it. The penalty is that we are to be cast away from God's presence and to perish without hope, as far as that broken covenant is concerned.

Now, rolling up that old covenant as a useless thing out of which no salvation can ever develop, God comes to us in another way and says, "I will make a new covenant with you, not like the old one at all." (See Hebrews 8:8–13.) It is a covenant of grace, a covenant made, not with the worthy, but with the unworthy; a covenant not made upon conditions, but unconditionally, every supposed condition having been fulfilled by our great Representative and Surety, the Lord Jesus

Christ; a covenant without an *if* or a *but* in it; *"an everlasting covenant, ordered in all things, and sure"* (2 Samuel 23:5); a covenant of *shalls* and *wills,* in which God says, "I will, and you shall"; a covenant suited to our broken-down, helpless condition; a covenant that will land everyone who has an interest in it in heaven. No other covenant will ever do this.

In earlier chapters, I discussed the covenant of grace. Now I would like to show to any who desire to be in this covenant of grace what the blessings are that God promises to give to guilty men when they come to Him, when they accept His love and His mercy. What are these blessings? I have little else to do but to refer you again to God's Word.

Beloved, if you had met together after the death of some wealthy relative and his will were about to be read to you, you would not require an eloquent lawyer. You would all be very attentive, and some of you who are a little deaf would recover your hearing. An important question would be, What has he bequeathed? A still more important inquiry would be, What has he left to me?

I hope you feel right now that you do not want an eloquent teacher, because I am only going to read God's will with you, His covenant, which is virtually the testament or will of Christ. All that you have to do is to pay attention and say, "What has He left? What has He bequeathed to me? What did He covenant to give to me?"

Twelve Covenant Mercies

Remember that, whoever you may be, if you are willing to be saved by grace, you may be saved by grace. If you give up all hope of being saved any other way, you may be saved by the free mercy and love of God. *"If ye be willing and obedient, ye shall eat the good of the land"* (Isaiah 1:19). If you come and take Christ as your Savior, then *"all the promises of God* [which] *in him are yea, and in him Amen"* (2 Corinthians 1:20) are made to you. If you take Him, you take all that is in the covenant, for He is the covenant. Embodied in Him is the whole covenant of grace, and the person who has Christ has all it contains.

I am simply going to point out to you some of the passages in which we have this covenant written out at length. I will not say much about any one promise, but I will refer you to twelve wonderful mercies of the covenant of grace. Kindly look up each Scripture in your Bibles as we progress through these passages so that you may see for yourself.

As an aside, no music is more sweet to a gospel preacher than the rustle of Bible pages in the congregation. Many times when I have been in the pulpit and I have read a passage of Scripture, nobody has followed me to see if I was quoting correctly. I strongly urge you to take your Bibles with you when you go to church. What is the best way of hearing the Word? Is it not to search and see whether what the preacher says is really according to the Word of God? Thus, I entreat you to search the Scriptures to see if what is being taught to you is true. (See Acts 17:11.)

Saving Knowledge

The first mercy of the covenant we will look at is that of saving knowledge. Let us read from Jeremiah:

Behold, the days come, saith the LORD, That I will make a new covenant with the house of Israel, and with the house of Judah: not according to the covenant that I made with their fathers in the day that I took them by the hand to bring them out of the land of Egypt; which my covenant they brake, although I was an husband unto them, saith the LORD: But this shall be the covenant that I will make with the house of Israel; after those days, saith the LORD, I will put my law in their inward parts, and write it in their hearts; and will be their God, and they shall be my people. And they shall teach no more every man his neighbour, and every man his brother, saying, Know the LORD: for they shall all know me, from the least of them unto the greatest of them, saith the LORD: For I will forgive their iniquity, and I will remember their sin no more. (Jeremiah 31:31–34)

Saving knowledge is one of the first blessings of the covenant of grace. By nature, man does not know God; he does not want to know God; and when he is inspired to think of God at all, God seems a great mystery, a being invisible and unreasonable. The man asks, "Who will make me able to know God?" It may be that he reads his Bible, but even that he does not understand. He hears the preacher, but the Lord's servant seems to talk a jargon that the unconverted man cannot comprehend.

Twelve Covenant Mercies

Beloved, there is no knowing God except through God. A man's neighbor cannot teach him, even though he may attempt it. Though the neighbor may say, *"Know the LORD,"* yet he cannot give knowledge of God. By nature, our eyes are blinded; we cannot see. You may hold an electric light to a blind man's sightless orbs, but it will not give him sight. Blind Bartimaeus saw no light until Jesus spoke to him. (See Mark 10:46–52.) By his bigotry and self-righteousness, Saul of Tarsus was blind enough, until God shone a glorious light into his soul.

Now, here is a covenant that God will give the knowledge of Himself to the lost, the guilty, the ruined, to those who have provoked Him and gone astray from Him. Who, reading this, are those to whom this covenant will be fulfilled right now? I cannot tell except by marks and tokens, and this is one of the marks: Do you know that you are blind? Do you know that you cannot see apart from divine grace? Do you long to see? He is not totally blind, in a spiritual sense, who knows that he is so. He is not in the dark who senses that he is in the dark, because there is already some degree of light that makes him perceive the presence of darkness.

> **By nature, man does not know God and does not want to know God.**

O soul, if you desire to know God, here is the covenant: *"They shall all know me, from the least of them unto the greatest of them"* (Jeremiah 31:34). All God's chosen will know Him. Not one will abide in ignorance, neither will they die in ignorance. They will come to know the Lord and will *"grow in grace, and in the knowledge of our Lord and Saviour Jesus Christ"* (2 Peter 3:18). What a privilege this is!

"If any of you lack wisdom, let him ask of God, that giveth to all men liberally, and upbraideth not; and it shall be given him" (James 1:5). If any person is ignorant of God, let him hear the Word of the Lord, and let him seek the Lord. God will give him instruction concerning Himself and will make that person to know the great Jehovah, the Father of our spirits, who passes over iniquity, transgression, and sin.

God's Law Written in Men's Hearts

I must not linger on any one blessing. The first covenant mercy is saving knowledge; the next is that God's law will be written in the hearts of men. Let us read Jeremiah 31:33 again: *"After those days, saith the LORD, I will put my law in their inward parts, and write it in their hearts; and will be their God, and they shall be my people."*

You know that the Law of Moses was written on two tablets of stone. Wonderfully precious those two slabs of marble must have been when the divine finger had traced the solemn lines. Moses had a great charge to keep when he had those two divinely-written tablets, but he broke them because the people had broken them in spirit. It could not be that such divine writing should ever be handled or looked at by such an unholy people.

Now, friends, it was of no use writing the Commandments on tablets of stone except to serve as a condemnation of the people. However, when God comes in the covenant of grace, He does not merely give us the law in a book—the law written in legible characters—but He comes and writes on the fleshly tablets of our hearts. That way, the man knows the law by heart. What is even better, he loves the law. That law accuses him, but he would not have it altered. He bows and confesses the truthfulness of the accusation. He cries, "Lord, have mercy upon me, that You may incline my heart unto Yourself, to walk in all Your ways, and to keep Your commandments and Your statutes." (See 1 Kings 8:58.) This is the covenant blessing: God makes men to love His commandments and to delight themselves in truth, righteousness, and holiness.

A very wonderful thing is this writing on our hearts. Nobody but God can write on human hearts. I can write certain thoughts upon your minds as I appeal to your eyes and ears, but to get at the heart is another thing. Only He who has the keys of heaven, He who has the keys of the heart, He who shuts and no man opens, or opens and no man shuts (Revelation 3:7), only He can really get at the human heart. Yet, God does so get at the human heart that He writes His commandments there. Moreover, He does this to men who formerly hated those commandments; He makes them love His law. He makes men who despised His commandments

In the covenant of grace, God writes on the fleshly tablets of our hearts.

honor them. As for men who forgot His commandments, He writes them in their hearts so that they cannot get away from them. As for men who would have changed the commandments, He changes their hearts instead. Then their hearts and the commandments agree together.

This is a second covenant blessing. Do any of you want them? Would you like to know the Lord? Do you wish to have His law written on your hearts? *"According to your faith be it unto you"* (Matthew 9:29). Believe that God can do this for you, trust in Christ that it may be done unto you, and even so shall it be.

Free Pardon

The third covenant mercy is free pardon. You will find this at the end of Jeremiah 31:34: *"For I will forgive their iniquity, and I will remember their sin no more."* This is such a great blessing of the covenant. You people who think that you have never sinned, you who believe yourselves to have been always good—or at least as good as you could be—and far above the average of mankind, you exceedingly excellent people, who have never done anything that you need to repent of very greatly, I have nothing for you here. Only remember what Mary sang: *"He hath filled the hungry with good things;*

and the rich [that is you] *he hath sent empty away"* (Luke 1:53).

However, if one of you feels the burden of his guilt, if one soul is bowed down with grief because of the heavy load of past iniquity that lies upon it, surely, if you have the faith, you will jump for joy as you read these words: *"I will forgive their iniquity, and I will remember their sin no more."* First, the Lord will forgive and blot it out. He calls you by name and says, "Be as if you had never offended. Come to Me, come to My heart, as if you had always loved Me. Guilty though you are, I will not impute iniquity to your charge. I forgive it all." The great Judge will put on the white gloves, signifying mercy, and not the black cap, which indicates a death sentence. You are forgiven.

Then the Lord says, *"I will remember their sin no more."* It is a wonderful thing when omnipotence overcomes omniscience, when omnipotent love will not allow omniscience to recall: *"I will remember their sin no more."* Satan comes and pleads against the sinner, "God, this man did so-and-so." God says, "I do not remember it." And He does not remember it because He laid it all on Christ. Christ has suffered the penalty due for it, and therefore it is gone. It will never be recalled; it does not stand in the book of remembrance. As the Lord looks over this man's life, when He comes to the black pages, they are blank. Not a line is left, for He who died has made the scarlet sins as white as snow (Isaiah 1:18). *"I will remember their sin no more."*

Oh, what a precious covenant mercy is this! I do not feel as if I want to elaborate or embellish it in any way or give you any illustrations or tell you any anecdotes. Was there ever set before you such a glorious gift? Will you accept it, the perfect pardon of every sin and a divine act of amnesty and oblivion for every crime of every sort, published in the covenant of grace to every soul that is willing to receive it through Christ Jesus the Savior?

Reconciliation

Let us look a little farther to find something more. In Jeremiah 32:38 we read, *"And they shall be my people, and I will be their God."* Reconciliation is the next covenant mercy. The offense is put away; the sin is pardoned. "Now," says God, *"they shall be my people."*

"But, Lord, they are the people who worshipped Baal; they are the horrid wretches who gave their children up to be burned in the red-hot arms of Molech," someone objects.

"Nevertheless," says the Lord, *"they shall be my people."*

"But, Lord, these are the men and women who committed adultery and fornication, and were even guilty of murder."

"They shall be my people," says the Lord.

"But, Lord, they provoked You to anger year after year and would not listen to Your prophets."

Twelve Covenant Mercies

"They shall be my people," says the Lord, *"and I will be their God."*

Did you ever think how much there is involved in that expression, *"I will be their God"*? God is everything. When God gives Himself to us, He gives us more than all time and all eternity, all earth and all heaven. *"Fear not, Abram,"* said the Lord to the patriarch, *"I am thy shield, and thy exceeding great reward"* (Genesis 15:1), as if it were reward enough for any man to have God to be his God— and so it is. More riches than Croesus, more honor than the greatest conqueror, has the man who has this God to be his God forever and ever.

> **As the Lord looks over a forgiven sinner's life, when He comes to the black pages, they are blank.**

"And they shall be my people, and I will be their God." You might look that promise up and find how many times it occurs in the Word of God. I know that many times God puts it similarly: *"And they shall be my people, and I will be their God."* This is another grand covenant blessing.

Are you willing to be the people of God? Are you willing to take Him, even this God, to be yours forever and ever? If so, then our chapter text is true concerning you: *"I will make an everlasting covenant with you, even the sure mercies of David."*

True Godliness

Will you follow me to the next verse for a fifth covenant mercy, the blessing of true godliness? *"And I will give them one heart, and one way, that they may fear me for ever, for the good of them, and of their children after them"* (Jeremiah 32:39). Do you see here that *"the fear of the LORD is the beginning of wisdom"* (Proverbs 9:10)?

"The fear of the LORD" is a description of true godliness, and God says that He will give this to men. He might have asked it of you—and rightly, too—but you could never have produced it on your own. However, when He says that He will give it, that is a very different thing. He is willing to give you fear of Him, to give you true religion, to bestow upon you that veneration of His sacred name that lies at the bottom of all godliness.

God will give His fear to you who never had it, or even despised it, and to any of you who have lived all your lives without it but who are willing to come and take it, right now, as the gift of His grace through Jesus Christ. May the Lord make you *"willing in the day of* [His] *power"* (Psalm 110:3), for that is a part of the covenant blessing! The willingness itself is His gift, and this He gives freely to His own.

Continuance in Grace

Now look, dear friends, at the next verse, which is more wonderful than anything that I have yet read.

Twelve Covenant Mercies

In it we find the sixth covenant mercy, continuance in grace:

> *And I will make an everlasting covenant with them,*
> *that I will not turn away from them, to do them good;*
> *but I will put my fear in their hearts, that they shall not*
> *depart from me.* (Jeremiah 32:40)

Perseverance to the end, is it not granted here? *"I will not turn away from them...*[and] *they shall not depart from me."* What a covenant blessing this is! It reminds me of the words of the Lord Jesus concerning His sheep: *"And I give unto them eternal life; and they shall never perish, neither shall any man pluck them out of my hand"* (John 10:28).

A man who did not believe what that verse teaches said to me, "Well, no man may be able to pluck them out of His hand, but they can crawl away from between His fingers." No, they will not. See how this text secures them both ways: *"I will not turn away from them, to do them good; but I will put my fear in their hearts, that they shall not depart from me."* Here both gaps are blocked; there is no getting out either way. God will not leave you, and He will not let you leave Him. This is a covenant blessing indeed. Oh, for faith to lay hold of it! The soul who comes to Christ and rests wholly on Him will find two hands with which to grasp these two gracious words: *"I will not turn away from them,"* and *"they shall not depart from me."* And this is spoken of the guilty, of the very men who provoked God.

Grace

**Wonders of grace to God belong,
Repeat His mercies in your song.**

If God saved the good, the meritorious, and the righteous, then the proud Pharisees would swarm over every street in heaven, and God would have no glory. But, since He saves the vilest of the vile, the publicans, who are afraid to lift their eyes to heaven whenever they think of their own unworthiness, gather near the throne and sing of His free grace and dying love!

This covenant would be great enough if there were nothing more in it than the six blessings that I have already mentioned, but there are more. Let us look at another prophetic Scripture in order to read about more of the mercies of this covenant:

> *Then will I sprinkle clean water upon you, and ye shall be clean: from all your filthiness, and from all your idols, will I cleanse you. A new heart also will I give you, and a new spirit will I put within you: and I will take away the stony heart out of your flesh, and I will give you an heart of flesh. And I will put my spirit within you, and cause you to walk in my statutes, and ye shall keep my judgments, and do them. And ye shall dwell in the land that I gave to your fathers; and ye shall be my people, and I will be your God....Then shall ye remember your own evil ways, and your doings that were not good, and shall loathe yourselves in your own sight for your iniquities and for your abominations.*
> (Ezekiel 36:25–28, 31)

Twelve Covenant Mercies

Cleansing

In the above passage we find the seventh covenant mercy, namely that of cleansing. I can hear some poor soul saying, "Well, I can see that God is going to do great things, but I feel that I am so unclean I dare not come near to God. Why, I am polluted all over, inside and out. I am altogether like a leprous man!" Come then, let me read this verse to you: *"Then will I sprinkle clean water upon you, and ye shall be clean: from all your filthiness, and from all your idols, will I cleanse you."*

God's Word elsewhere commands, *"Wash you, make you clean"* (Isaiah 1:16). That is your duty. However, here you are told that the Lord will wash you and make you clean. This is your privilege. *"Ye are clean,"* said Christ to His disciples, *"through the word which I have spoken unto you"* (John 15:3). That is *"the washing of water by the word"* (Ephesians 5:26) of which Paul wrote to the church at Ephesus.

> **God will not leave you, and He will not let you leave Him.**

The free-grace covenant runs like this: *"Then will I sprinkle clean water upon you, and ye shall be clean."* The Lord sprinkles this *"clean water"* on the leprous and the polluted sinner, on the man who lies covered with his own blood, a filthy thing in the sight of God and loathsome to Him. When God Himself says, *"Ye shall be clean,"* I know that we are clean, for He is the best judge of true cleanliness. His pure and holy eyes detect every spot of sin and every latent trace of disease. Though it may be deep within the heart, He can spy it out; but He says, "I will sprinkle you, and you shall be clean."

Then the Lord goes on to enumerate that from which He will cleanse us: *"From all your idols, will I cleanse you."* Is drink your idol? Is some lust of the flesh your idol? "Oh!" you say, "I cannot get rid of these things." No, but the Lord can cleanse you from them. Only come to Him, listen diligently to Him, trust Him, yield to Him, surrender yourself to Him, and He will dash your idols in pieces and tear them from their thrones. He will also cleanse you from whatever else there may be that is unmentionable: *"from all your filthiness,"* things not to be spoken of, not even to be mentioned, those things that are done in secret. "I will cleanse you from them," says the Lord.

I may be addressing somebody who, as he reads this, thinks that I am delusional. "Why," says he, "I am a filthy creature. I am a great sinner. Can God bless me?" Yes, He can bless even you.

Such was the case of Colonel Gardiner. On the very night on which he had made an appointment to commit a filthy sin, Christ appeared to him, and he thought that he heard Him say, "I have done all this for you; will you never turn to Me?" At that moment he did turn to Jesus. He became noted as an eminent Christian man, more noted than he had formerly been as a debauched officer in the army.

Twelve Covenant Mercies

The Lord Jesus Christ still works these wonders of grace. He meets men often when they are desperately set on mischief, just as a horse that is rushing head-long into battle. Christ comes and lays His hand on the reins, turns the steed, and leads it back wherever He desires. Such is the power of His almighty love. I pray that He will do the same for you, according to this wondrous promise: *"Then will I sprinkle clean water upon you, and ye shall be clean: from all your filthiness, and from all your idols, will I cleanse you."*

A Renewed Nature

Nor is that all. When a man is once made clean, he would soon become foul again if left to himself. So, here follows the next astounding covenant mercy, a renewal of nature.

> *A new heart also will I give you, and a new spirit will I put within you: and I will take away the stony heart out of your flesh, and I will give you an heart of flesh.*
> (Ezekiel 36:26)

God did not say, "I will help you to this," but, "I will do it." His words were not, "I will help you to make yourself a new heart"—no, nothing of the kind—but, "I will give you a new heart."

You know that if you cut off the branches of a tree, it will grow fresh ones. However, if you could tear out its heart, it would never grow a new one. There are some creatures such as the lobster that will shed their claws, and the claws will grow again, but a lobster can never grow a new heart. If the center of animal or vegetable life is once destroyed, there is no renewing it. Even so, God can work this miracle in human hearts. He can strike at the very center of man's nature and change it. It takes little to purify the flowing streams, but it is a great marvel to cleanse an impure spring so that the bitter water suddenly turns sweet. This is a miracle that can only be brought about by the finger of God, yet there is nothing except this renewal of the inward nature that is worth having.

God can strike at the very center of man's nature and change it.

Some people imagine that we Christians, when we do not attend or participate in certain worldly amusements, are very much denying ourselves. It is nothing of the kind. Contrary to their thinking, it would be an awful denial for us if we had to go with the worldlings to pollute our minds and hearts with their loose amusements. Those who frequent such places perhaps assume that it is a denial for us not to go with them. How little they know us!

When I go down to a friend's farm, I see a man carrying a couple of pails full of food to the pigs, but I never envy the pigs. I like them to have all that they can and to enjoy themselves, but do not suppose that I am denying myself in not wanting their food. My taste does not lie that way.

Twelve Covenant Mercies

But, suppose that a man has a hog's heart. What is the way to deal with him—to deny him his swill? Certainly not, let him have it while he is like the hogs. The thing that is needed is a change of heart. When his heart is turned into a renewed man's heart and is made to be a godlike heart, then it is no denial to him to loathe the things that once gave him so much pleasure. His tastes are entirely changed, according to the promise of the covenant: *"A new heart also will I give you, and a new spirit will I put within you."*

The old heart is very hard. In some poor souls, it seems to be altogether petrified. You cannot make any impression upon it. You are received with ridicule, however earnest you may be in your testimonies for God. Yet, the Lord can change that stony heart to a heart of flesh.

> **Our heart, that flinty, stubborn thing,**
> **That terrors cannot move,**
> **That fears no threat'nings of His wrath,**
> **Shall be dissolved by love.**
> **Or he can take the flint away,**
> **That would not be refined;**
> **And from the treasures of His grace,**
> **Bestow a softer mind.**

Then the man, who had just previously been as hard as flint, sits and weeps over his sins. See how watchful he is in the presence of all kinds of temptations. He is half afraid to put one foot in front of the other. The very man with the devil-may-care attitude is now the one who does care and who trembles lest he should in any way grieve the living God. What a blessed covenant mercy is this!

Holy Conduct

Moving on, we find that the ninth covenant mercy is holy conduct. Let us continue reading in Ezekiel:

And I will put my spirit within you, and cause you to walk in my statutes, and ye shall keep my judgments, and do them. (Ezekiel 36:27)

When God deals with a man through His grace, He not only calls him to holiness, but He gives him holiness; He not only bids him walk in His way, but He makes him walk in His way. He does so, not by compulsion, not by any kind of physical force, but by the sweet constraints of infinite love. The man's entire life is changed externally, just as I have shown you that his heart is changed internally. "Oh," says one, "this is very wonderful!" Yes, it is the steadfast wonder of the Gospel. Certain miracles may have ceased, but the miracles of turning men from darkness to light and from the power of Satan to the power of God are being accomplished every day.

I rejoice that they are constantly being brought about in houses of prayer around the world, and I believe that they are going to be produced in some who are now reading this book. If this miracle is accomplished, do not attribute it to me, for I ask you to remember how feeble I am. Rather, understand that the power of God works through the teaching of the Gospel, making dry bones live and turning black sinners into bright saints, to the praise of the glory of His grace.

Happy Self-Loathing

This will be the tenth covenant mercy, happy self-loathing. Perhaps you wonder that I called this a mercy. But, read the following:

> *Then shall ye remember your own evil ways, and your doings that were not good, and shall loathe yourselves in your own sight for your iniquities and for your abominations.* (Ezekiel 36:31)

Free grace makes men loathe themselves. After God has done so much for them, they feel so ashamed that they do not know what to do. "O Lord," says the saint, "to think that I could have ever sinned against One who loved me so much! That I, the elect of God, could have ever acted like the elect of hell! That I, who am Your own, ever called myself the devil's own! That I, who was chosen unto holiness and eternal life, passed it all by as if it were no concern of mine!" May God grant us this holy loathing, as He will do when we have once tasted of His infinite love!

God not only bids us to walk in His way but makes us to do so by the sweet constraints of infinite love.

Communion with God

The next covenant mercy, mentioned in Ezekiel chapter 37, is the blessing of communion with God:

Moreover I will make a covenant of peace with them; it shall be an everlasting covenant with them: and I will place them, and multiply them, and will set my sanctuary in the midst of them for evermore. My tabernacle also shall be with them: yea, I will be their God, and they shall be my people. And the heathen shall know that I the LORD do sanctify Israel, when my sanctuary shall be in the midst of them for evermore.

(Ezekiel 37:26–28)

God promises to set up His tabernacle and His temple in the midst of His people and to make them His priests, His servants, His children, His friends. God will no longer be absent from you when this covenant work has been accomplished in you. You will be brought to dwell in His presence, to abide in His house, no more to go out, until the day when He takes you to His palace home above to be forever in His presence and to serve Him in His temple. All this is promised to the worthless, to the most vile; all this without asking of you anything but that you will be willing to receive Him; all this without requiring of you anything but just your emptiness that He may fill it, your sinfulness that He may cleanse it, and your surrender to Him. What have you to surrender? Nothing but

Free grace makes men loathe themselves.

a lot of rubbish of your own—your self-righteousness especially, which is but *"filthy rags"* (Isaiah 64:6) to Him. May the Lord bring you to this surrender even now!

Necessary Chastisement

There is one more covenant mercy for me to mention, and I put it last because you will be surprised, perhaps, when I state it. It is about needed chastisement. For this I ask you to turn to Psalm 89:

> *If his children forsake my law, and walk not in my judgments; if they break my statutes, and keep not my commandments; then will I visit their transgression with the rod, and their iniquity with stripes. Nevertheless my lovingkindness will I not utterly take from him, nor suffer my faithfulness to fail.* (Psalm 89:30–33)

There is a rod of grace in the covenant. Children of God, you do not like it; it would be no rod if you did. However, it is good for you when you come under the fatherly discipline of God. Though He will never take His everlasting love from you nor suffer His faithfulness to fail, yet when you transgress, His rod will be sure to fall upon you. Sometimes its strokes will come upon you before you transgress to keep you from sinning.

> **You will be brought to dwell in God's presence, no more to go out.**

I often hear of some of God's dearest servants suffering. I heard of one whom I am sure God loves very much. He is very useful in the Lord's kingdom and spends himself in his Master's work. He is also very prosperous; God has given to him great wealth that he discreetly and wisely uses. With all of that, however, he has had a very sharp affliction come upon him lately that is enough to break his heart. When I heard about it, I said, "Yes, yes, God loves him; God loves him."

If you are a child of God, note this truth, and accept it with joy: Our heavenly Father never pampers His children. We may spoil our sons and daughters, but our Father never spoils His children. If He gives you great happiness and great success and makes you useful, He will every now and then give you a whipping behind the door.

> **Our heavenly Father never pampers His children.**

You may think sometimes, "That man is very happy; he has great blessing resting on his work." Yes, this man is very happy to tell you that he does not have all sweets to drink, which would make him weak and sickly; but there are bitter tonics in his life, sharp blows of the rod, to keep him right. If we have to bless God more for any one thing than for everything else, it is to thank Him that we have not escaped the rod. Infirmity can be a choice blessing from God. I cannot measure the unutterable good that comes to us often in that way. Losses in business and crosses and bereavements and depressions of spirit are all so many covenant mercies when we see them in the light of eternity.

Twelve Covenant Mercies

The true-born child of God cannot escape the rod and would not if he could. He gets afraid when he does not sometimes feel it. He will not long have to be afraid about it, for it will come in due time.

I think that I hear somebody say, "I do not want that." Rightly said, because you want worldly pleasure. Perhaps God will let you have it until you have spent all your substance on it, as the prodigal did. Then you will find that it is all weariness and sorrow, and you will want something better.

However, if you will say, "I will take the covenant of grace, rod and all; for if I can be God's child, I will very gladly take the rod as part of the mercies of the covenant," come, and you shall have it. Do seek the Lord this moment. Do not give sleep to your eyes nor allow your eyelids to close until you have found Him.

May God grant you all the mercies of the everlasting covenant, for Jesus' sake! Amen.

About the Author
Charles Haddon Spurgeon

C harles Haddon Spurgeon was born on June 19, 1834 at Kelvedon, Essex, England, the firstborn of eight surviving children. His parents were committed Christians, and his father was a preacher. Spurgeon was converted in 1850 at the age of fifteen. He began to help the poor and to hand out tracts and was known as "The Boy Preacher."

His next six years were eventful. He preached his first sermon at the age of sixteen. At age eighteen, he became the pastor of Waterbeach Baptist Chapel, preaching in a barn. Spurgeon preached over six hundred times before he reached the age of twenty. By

1854, he was well-known and was asked to become the pastor of New Park Street Chapel in London. In 1856, Spurgeon married Susannah Thompson; they had twin sons, both of whom later entered the ministry.

Spurgeon's compelling sermons and lively preaching style drew multitudes of people, and many came to Christ. Soon, the crowds had grown so large that they blocked the narrow streets near the church. Services eventually had to be held in rented halls, and Spurgeon often preached to congregations of more than ten thousand. The Metropolitan Tabernacle was built in 1861 to accommodate the large numbers of people.

Spurgeon published over two thousand sermons, which were so popular that they literally sold by the ton. At one point, his sermons sold twenty-five thousand copies every week. An 1870 edition of the English magazine *Vanity Fair* called him an "original and powerful preacher...honest, resolute, sincere; lively, entertaining." He appealed constantly to his hearers to move on in the Christian faith, to allow the Lord to minister to them individually, and to be used by God to win the lost to Christ. His sermons were scripturally inspiring and highlighted with flashes of spontaneous and delightful humor. The prime minister of England, members of the royal family, and Florence Nightingale, among others, went to hear him preach. Spurgeon preached to an estimated ten million people throughout his life. Not surprisingly, he is called the "Prince of Preachers."

About the Author

In addition to his powerful preaching, Spurgeon founded and supported charitable outreaches, including educational institutions. His pastors' college, which is still in existence today, taught nearly nine hundred students in Spurgeon's time. He also founded the famous Stockwell Orphanage.

In his later years, Spurgeon often publicly disagreed with the emergence of modern biblical criticism that led the believer away from a total dependence on the Word of God.

Charles Spurgeon died at Mentone, France, in 1892, leaving a legacy of writings to the believer who seeks to know the Lord Jesus more fully.

Steps to Peace With God

1. God's Purpose: Peace and Life

God loves you and wants you to experience peace and life—abundant and eternal.

The Bible Says ...

"We have peace with God through our Lord Jesus Christ." *Romans 5:1, NIV*

"For God so loved the world that He gave His only begotten Son, that whoever believes in Him should not perish but have everlasting life." *John 3:16, NKJV*

"I have come that they may have life, and that they may have it more abundantly." *John 10:10, NKJV*

Since God planned for us to have peace and the abundant life right now, why are most people not having this experience?

2. Our Problem: Separation From God

God created us in His own image to have an abundant life. He did not make us as robots to automatically love and obey Him, but gave us a will and a freedom of choice.

We chose to disobey God and go our own willful way. We still make this choice today. This results in separation from God.

The Bible Says ...

"For all have sinned and fall short of the glory of God." *Romans 3:23, NIV*

"For the wages of sin is death, but the gift of God is eternal life in Christ Jesus our Lord." *Romans 6:23, NIV*

Our choice results in separation from God.

OUR ATTEMPTS

Through the ages, individuals have tried in many ways to bridge this gap ... without success ...

THE BIBLE SAYS ...

"There is a way that seems right to a man, but in the end it leads to death."
Proverbs 14:12, NIV

"But your iniquities have separated you from your God; and your sins have hidden His face from you, so that He will not hear."
Isaiah 59:2, NKJV

There is only one remedy for this problem of separation.

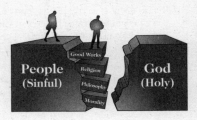

3. GOD'S REMEDY: THE CROSS

Jesus Christ is the only answer to this problem. He died on the cross and rose from the grave, paying the penalty for our sin and bridging the gap between God and people.

THE BIBLE SAYS ...

"For there is one God and one mediator between God and men, the man Christ Jesus."
1 Timothy 2:5, NIV

"For Christ also suffered once for sins, the just for the unjust, that He might bring us to God."
1 Peter 3:18, NKJV

"But God demonstrates His own love toward us, in that while we were still sinners, Christ died for us." *Romans 5:8, NKJV*

God has provided the only way ... we must make the choice ...

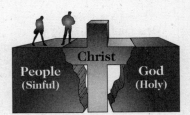

4. Our Response: Receive Christ

We must trust Jesus Christ and receive Him by personal invitation.

The Bible Says ...

"Behold, I stand at the door and knock. If anyone hears My voice and opens the door, I will come in to him and dine with him, and he with Me." *Revelation 3:20, NKJV*

"But as many as received Him, to them He gave the right to become children of God, to those who believe in His name." *John 1:12, NKJV*

"If you confess with your mouth the Lord Jesus and believe in your heart that God has raised Him from the dead, you will be saved." *Romans 10:9, NKJV*

Are you here ... or here?

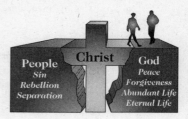

Is there any good reason why you cannot receive Jesus Christ right now?

How To Receive Christ:

1. Admit your need (say, "I am a sinner").
2. Be willing to turn from your sins (repent) and ask for God's forgiveness.
3. Believe that Jesus Christ died for you on the cross and rose from the grave.
4. Through prayer, invite Jesus Christ to come in and control your life through the Holy Spirit (receive Jesus as Lord and Savior).

What To Pray:

Dear Lord Jesus,
    I know that I am a sinner, and I ask for Your forgiveness. I believe You died for my sins and rose from the dead. I turn from my sins and invite You to come into my heart and life. I want to trust and follow You as my Lord and Savior.

In Your Name, Amen.

Date   Signature

GOD'S ASSURANCE: HIS WORD

IF YOU PRAYED THIS PRAYER,

THE BIBLE SAYS ...

"For, 'Everyone who calls on the name of the Lord will be saved.'"
Romans 10:13, NIV

Did you sincerely ask Jesus Christ to come into your life? Where is He right now? What has He given you?

"For it is by grace you have been saved, through faith—and this not from yourselves, it is the gift of God—not by works, so that no one can boast."
Ephesians 2:8–9, NIV

THE BIBLE SAYS ...

"He who has the Son has life; he who does not have the Son of God does not have life. These things I have written to you who believe in the name of the Son of God, that you may know that you have eternal life, and that you may continue to believe in the name of the Son of God."
1 John 5:12–13, NKJV

Receiving Christ, we are born into God's family through the supernatural work of the Holy Spirit who indwells every believer. This is called regeneration or the "new birth."

This is just the beginning of a wonderful new life in Christ. To deepen this relationship you should:

1. Read your Bible every day to know Christ better.
2. Talk to God in prayer every day.
3. Tell others about Christ.
4. Worship, fellowship, and serve with other Christians in a church where Christ is preached.
5. As Christ's representative in a needy world, demonstrate your new life by your love and concern for others.

God bless you as you do.

Billy Graham

If you want further help in the decision you have made, write to:
Billy Graham Evangelistic Association
1 Billy Graham Parkway, Charlotte, North Carolina 28201-0001